FOREX

FOR AMBITIOUS BEGINNERS

JELLE PETERS

A GUIDE TO SUCCESSFUL CURRENCY TRADING

ODYSSEA PUBLISHING

MARKETS.COM
WHERE THE WORLD COMES TO TRADE

Special promotion for readers of
Forex for Ambitious Beginners

Practice everything you've learned reading

"Forex for Ambitious Beginners"

with a **FREE €50 bonus**- no deposit required-

with Markets.com, one of Europe's leading Forex brokers.

Scan the QR code, or simply enter your
promo code at the registration page on
www.Markets.com

Promo code: 50NODEPOSIT

Trading with Markets.com you will also enjoy a complete
follow-up education program, zero commission trading and
industry tight spreads.

FOREX FOR AMBITIOUS BEGINNERS

© 2012 Odyssea Publishing

ISBN # 978-90-810821-4-3

www.forexforambitiousbeginners.com

Cover design & layout: ePUB Pro, Utrecht, The Netherlands. www.epubpro.nl

First Edition, July 2012
Second Edition, September 2014

TABLE OF CONTENTS

Introduction

Part I How the Forex Market Works
Part II Trading on the Forex Yourself
Part III Understanding and Predicting Price Movements
Part IV Forex Trading Strategies
Part V How to Become a Successful Forex Trader

Part VI Forex Quiz

TABLE OF CONTENTS

INTRODUCTION   15

HOW THE FOREX MARKET WORKS   17

CHAPTER 1 A SHORT HISTORY OF THE FOREIGN EXCHANGE MARKET   19
  Barter and the Beginnings of International Trade   19
  the Gold Standard   20
  Bretton Woods   21
  Birth of the Modern Currency Market   22
    The man who broke the bank of England
  the Future of the Forex   23

CHAPTER 2 PRACTICAL INFORMATION ABOUT THE FOREX   24
  What Is the Forex Exactly   24
  Opening Hours   24
    (rock) Around the clock
    The busy hours
  Who Is Active on the Forex   25
    Banks
    Multinationals
    Governments
    Individual Traders
  Regulations   28

CHAPTER 3 HOW CURRENCY RATES ARE DETERMINED   29
  Currency Pairs   29
  Opening a Position   30

CHAPTER 4 THE DIFFERENCE BETWEEN FOREX AND STOCKS   32
  Not an Investment Market But a Speculative Market   32
  Not Based on Physical Ownership   33
  Trading Stocks Is More Expensive   34
  Similarities   34
  Why Recessions Don't Matter to the Forex Trader   35
    No Uptick Rule

CHAPTER 5 INDIVIDUAL TRADERS ON THE FOREX   37
  Online Trading Platforms   37
  Start with a Small Trading Capital   38

CHAPTER 6 SHORT FOREX LEXICON   39
  Opening a Position   39
  Long or Short   39

Stop Loss   39
Take Profit   39
Bulls & Bears   40
Bid and Ask   40
Spread   40
Base Currency and Quote Currency   40
Cross Currencies   40
Candlestick Chart   41
Leverage   41
Standard Lot   42
Pip   42
Resistance and Support   42

TRADING ON THE FOREX YOURSELF   43

CHAPTER 7 YOUR FIRST FOREX ACCOUNT   45
  Required Trading Capital   45
  Choosing the Right Forex Broker   46
  Demo Account or Real Account?   47
  Opening Your First Position   48
  Money Management   49
  What Is a Realistic Return on Investment   51
  Automated Trading Yes or No?   51
    Your Own Expert Advisor
    Buying an Existing Expert Advisor / Forex Bot
  5 Tips that Will Save You Money   53
    1. Money Management
    2. Always Use a Stop Loss
    3. Be Realistic
    4. Interact with Other Traders
    5. Keep Your Emotions under Control

UNDERSTANDING AND PREDICTING PRICE MOVEMENTS   57

CHAPTER 8 THE FOUR MOST IMPORTANT CURRENCIES ON THE FOREX – AND THE
YUAN   59
  What Makes the US Dollar So Important   59
    The Federal Reserve
  Where Is the Chinese Yuan?   60
  the Euro   61
    European Central Bank
    EUR/USD
    Things You Should Know about the EUR/USD

Important Economic Indicators for the Euro Are:

Trading Opportunities for the EUR/USD

the Japanese Yen   64

Ministry of Finance and the Bank of Japan

Important Economic Indicators for the Yen:

USD/JPY

What Should You Pay Attention to When Trading the USD/JPY

the British Pound   66

Bank of England

GBP/USD

What Influences the Cable

The GBP/USD in Relation to Other Currency Pairs

Trading Opportunities for the GBP/USD

CHAPTER 10 FUNDAMENTAL ANALYSIS   69

Why Economic News Is Important   69

Forex Traders Big and Small React to Financial News Because:

Fundamental Analysis at Work   70

the Four Fundamental Themes Influencing the Forex   72

Economic Growth

Interest Rates

Trade Balance

Political Stability

Note

CHAPTER 11 TECHNICAL ANALYSIS   76

Charting and Judging Price Developments   76

Different Ways of Looking at Price Developments   77

The Development of the Price over Time

The Development of the Development of the Price over Time

The Development of the Price in Different Time Frames

Candlestick Charts   78

Some Examples of Candlesticks and Candlestick Patterns

   The Doji

   Three White Soldiers

   The Hammer

CHAPTER 12 CHART PATTERNS   80

Head-and-Shoulders   81

Triangle Pattern   83

Symmetrical Triangle

Rising Triangle

Falling Triangle

CHAPTER 13 SUPPORT AND RESISTANCE   86
  Causes of Support and Resistance Levels   87
  How to Use Support and Resistance   87
  Some Tips for Using Support and Resistance   88

CHAPTER 14 THE MOST IMPORTANT TECHNICAL INDICATORS   90
  Moving Averages   90
    SMA Derivative Indicators, Methods
      Exponential Moving Average (EMA)
      Moving Averages Crossover Systems
      3 SMA Filter
      Tight to Wide 3 SMA Trade
  Bollinger Bands   93
    Using Bollinger Bands to Open and Close Positions
      Trend Detection -- When Can We Say a Trend Is Emerging?
      Entry Point -- When to Open a Position?
      Exit Point -- When is the Trend Considered to Have Run Its Course?
  Relative Strength Index   96
    How the RSI Works
    How to Use the Relative Strength Index
    Divergence
  Stochastics   98
    Range Trading Tool
    Stochastics Explained
    Stochastics at its Best: Divergence
  Fibonacci   100
    So, Finally, What Is the Fibonacci Sequence
    How the Fibonacci Sequence Works in Trading
      Fibonacci Support Levels in an Uptrend
      Fibonacci Extension Ratios
    Why Fibonacci Is Important in FX Trading

FOREX TRADING STRATEGIES   105

CHAPTER 15 TREND TRADING   107
  What Is a Trend   107
  Trend Trading Strategy   108

CHAPTER 16 RANGE TRADING   110
  the Nuts and Bolts of Range Trading   110
  How to Recognize a Possible Range Trade   112
  How Do You Set Up a Range Trading Strategy   113
    Identify the Range
    Identify the Entry Point for the Trade (a.k.a. the Trigger)
    Set a Stop Loss and Profit Target

CHAPTER 17 SCALPING   115
  Not a Good Strategy for Beginners   115
  How Scalping Works   116
  Is Scalping the Holy Grail?   116

CHAPTER 18 BREAKOUT TRADING   117
  Example of a Breakout Strategy   117
  Different Kinds of Breakouts   118
  Testing a Breakout   119

CHAPTER 19 FADING THE BREAKOUT   121
  Example of Breakout Fading   121
  Short Term Trading Strategy   122

CHAPTER 20 THE CARRY TRADE   123
  How the Carry Trade Works   123
  Carry Trade Example   124
  How to Spot a Good Carry Trade   125
  Summary of the Carry Trade   125

CHAPTER 21 TRADING THE NEWS   127
  How to Trade the News   127
    5 Minute Charts
    Difference between Actual and Expected Figures
    Which Direction Is Not Important
    Clear Direction IS Important
    Tight Stops
    Trailing Stops
    Summary

HOW TO BECOME A SUCCESSFUL FOREX TRADER   131

CHAPTER 22 WHAT KIND OF TRADING IS RIGHT FOR YOU   134
  Goals   134
    Time
    Study
    Money
  Why Most Traders Lose Money   135
  Self-Assessment   136
  Trader X   138
    Trading Conditions Trader X

CHAPTER 23 SET-UPS   140
  Set-Up Example I: Bollinger Bands Breakout   140

Set-Up Example II: Sma Breakout   140
Why Use a Set-Up   141
A Good Set-Up Is Important for the Following Reasons:

CHAPTER 24 EXIT STRATEGY   143
Infamous Examples of the Lack of an Exit Strategy   143
Example 1 World vs. Credit Crisis
Example 2 the US vs. the Rest
Example 3 Oil Price vs. Hedge Funds
Exit Strategy to Limit Losses: the Stop Loss   144
Exit Strategy to Secure and Maximize Profits   145
Scaling Exit Points   146

CHAPTER 25 MONEY MANAGEMENT   148
Position Sizing   148
The Most Important Goals of Position Sizing
Protecting Your Trading Capital
Expected Value (EV) and Calculating Your Evp
Conclusion

CHAPTER 26 SYSTEM EVALUATION   152
the Numbers   152
Expected Value Expressed in Position Size (EVP)
Trading Capital Growth/Decline
Percentage Total Winning Trades
What to Evaluate and How Often   153
Evaluation of Your Trading System in Numbers
Evaluating Different Parts of Your Trading System
Trading Log   154
Example of a trading log

CHAPTER 27 THE PSYCHOLOGY OF TRADING   156
When You Should Not Trade   156
When You Shouldn't Trade a Little While Longer   157
Worst Case Scenario Strategy   157
Worst case scenario examples
Situation 1: Dramatic Losses
Situation 2: Girlfriend/Boyfriend Part I
Situation 3: No More Forex
Situation 4: Big Bad Government
Situation 5: Uptick Yourself
Situation 6: Girlfriend/Boyfriend Part II
Worst Case Scenario Tip for Beginning Traders   158
The End of the Beginning

FOREX QUIZ   161

ANSWERS QUIZ   175

EXPLANATION ANSWERS FOREX QUIZ   179

EXPLANATION QUIZ SCORES   205

SHORT FOREX LEXICON   209

BIBLIOGRAPHY   215

INTRODUCTION

The currency market (a.k.a foreign exchange, forex, FX) has been the fastest growing financial market of the past two decades and certainly also one of the most exciting ones. Since 2000 the daily transaction value at the forex has grown from $1,7 trillion to $3,98 trillion. That's 3,980 billion dollar, per day. By comparison, the average daily volume at the New York Stock Exchange, – the most important stock exchange in the world – was $153 billion in 2008; in other words, 1/26 part the forex.

Several factors contribute to the growing popularity of currency trading.

1. The internet. It's really no coincidence that currency trading has grown exponentially in the past decade. Thanks to the huge growth in the number of broadband connections, many individual consumers are now able to use the kind of online trading platforms that had previously only been available to professional traders working out of dealing rooms.
2. An increased willingness to take risks. This new generation of traders is more comfortable taking risks in exchange for a chance at bigger gains, and faster turn around on their investments.
3. Low start-up costs. The forex trading game is open even to people with only a couple of hundred bucks to trade with. Try opening an equity account at your bank with just $100!
4. Low operation costs. Trading currency is cheaper, much cheaper, than trading stocks. Forex brokers don't charge commission, only spread, making it a particularly interesting proposition for small traders.
5. Instant gratification. 'Now' is the new magic word in trading as well as in everything else. The forex is open 24 hours a day, five days a week, and is therefore much better equipped to cater to the needs of the 'I want it now' generation than stock markets, which are only open for a couple of hours a day. People don't want to be dependant anymore on opening hours, or wait for investing opportunities that present themselves only once or twice a month.

Now, chances are that you've already heard some great stories about how easy it is to make money trading on the forex. Maybe you heard a story about a beginning trader just like you, who started out with just a couple of hundred bucks and with this or that simple strategy and made tens of thousands of dollars in profit in only a few months.

Yeah, that's not gonna happen.

I don't want to burst your bubble or anything, but it's better to start out with your feet firmly planted on the road to riches and not have your head filled with fantasies. The latter will only bring you unnecessary disappointment. Sure, for every trading strategy there is one happy idiot who made a bundle using it. This kind of luck can be seen at work in the lottery as well. As you have bought this book I take it you're not interested in the ins & outs of a lottery (a losing proposition by the way) but want to learn about how to make money consistently trading currencies. And 'consistent' is one word 'luck' will never be friends with.

You should therefore realize the following truth: trading the forex is not a 'get rich quick scheme'. When you first start out trading the currency market, you will make errors. You will take on too much risk, forget to set your stop/loss, practice bad money management, lack an exit strategy, etc. Every beginner makes mistakes, it's only natural; the question is how many mistakes, how much will they cost you, and what are you going to learn from them.

This book won't make you rich, but it can quickly teach you a lot about how the forex works, what the most important trading strategies are, how you can protect your trading capital and how to avoid many, many, mistakes. In short, this book will send you off to a flying start as a forex trader.

After reading *Forex for Ambitious Beginners* you'll have an advantage over 95% of those other beginning FX traders -- those unprepared and ill equipped people who got in over their heads and were never heard from again.

So congratulations with this excellent head start and all the best wishes for the rest of your forex trading career!

Jelle Peters

P.S. Please visit www.forexforambitiousbeginners.com if you have any questions about the book or the quiz.

PART I

HOW THE FOREX MARKET WORKS

CHAPTER 1 A SHORT HISTORY OF THE FOREIGN EXCHANGE MARKET

To better understand how the currency market works, it's important to know a little bit about its history. For instance, what is the *Gold Standard* and does it still play a role in today's fast and fluid financial world? How long has the forex existed in its current form? And who or what makes sure that everything at the forex happens according to regulations? What kind of regulations would that be by the way? And while we're playing 20 questions, why is the US Dollar so omnipresent on the forex? (the USD is present in all five of the most important currency pairs)

Extra: The value of a given currency compared to another currency is acquired by trading it against that other currency in a 'currency pair'. The five most important currency pairs are the EUR/USD | GBP/USD | USD/JPY | USD/CHF | USD/CAD. More about this in chapter 3 'How currency rates are determined'.

Another often heard question -- Why is a currency market even needed in the first place? Why not simply choose a fixed ratio between currencies? Wouldn't that be easier – not to mention cheaper and much more stable – than a (completely) free floating currency market?

To be sure, the forex in its current form – made up of currency pairs, with prices that are determined by the free market – is relatively new. It came into being only in the 1970s. However, when it comes to the international monetary system, the real champion of the last couple of thousand years has been gold, far and wide. A rare, universally coveted, natural currency that even in today's modern world is very much in demand in times of economic uncertainty.

BARTER AND THE BEGINNINGS OF INTERNATIONAL TRADE

Much to the dismay of Marxist idealists, barter only works in a very simple economy. That doesn't stop them from starting new initiatives in modern, capitalist economies to reintroduce barter, but it never goes anywhere outside the margins of very local ecosystems. (think: *wanted, repair of washing machine in exchange for slightly broken armoire*). Often, these initiatives accidentally stumble upon the very same idea they are trying to get away from, the idea of money (e.g. the repair of washing machine = 3 bitcoins a slightly broken armoire = 2 bitcoins, mowing the lawn = 4 bitcoins, etc)

So why didn't bartering make it into the modern world as the default payment system? Because it's hard enough to compare the value of a given product with the value of one other product, let alone 10,000 other products. As it turns out, the best and most effective way to do this is to find one product that everybody will always want to have. Amazing huh?

In the past, that product was often gold or silver, although there have been a number of other products that were used by various societies, such as salt, and seashells. In ancient China they used tea blocks[1], and in the Southern States of the US people regularly payed each other in tobacco.

One of the first examples of a coin that gained international acceptance was the Roman golden *Aureus*[2] – later followed by the silver *Denarius*. The international acceptance of these coins as valid currency was of course partly based on the intrinsic value of the material they were made of, but it was primarily the power and stability of the Roman Empire that made the coins a currency that was accepted even well beyond the borders of the empire.

Of course the problem with accepting a currency where it's not in use as the default currency is of course that it has to be exchanged into that default currency first. An American shopkeeper has no use for a British five pound note. He can't use it to buy a beer over at Barney's, across the street, so he won't accept it as payment himself.

Interestingly enough, American dollars and euro's are nowadays accepted in many countries where they are not the official currency. In that way, they're a bit like the golden Aureus. But for the most part their acceptance is limited to places that are frequented by a lot of foreigners, like airports and hotels.

THE GOLD STANDARD

During the first half of the nineteenth century, the United Kingdom[3] introduced the Gold Standard. A number of other countries followed after 1870. In a system that uses the Gold Standard, a fixed weight in gold is set for the currency, and the exchange of both coin and paper currency to gold is guaranteed by the state. Naturally, a system like this assures a great deal of monetary stability. People no longer had to fear their money rapidly loosing value, because it was now directly pegged to the value of gold, a rare commodity that had proven its value in the monetary system for ages.

The exchangeability of different currencies also became much easier thanks to the Gold Standard, since the guaranteed, underlying value for the currencies

---

1   In Tibet, Mongolia and Central-Asia, tea blocks were also in use as currency for centuries. In Siberia, for instance, tea blocks were accepted as payment until WW II.

2   The Aureus was issued from first century BC until the fourth century. 1 Aureus was worth 25 Denarii.

3   The Bank Charter Act of 1844 dictates that the monopoly of issuing bank notes will rest with the Bank of England; its notes are guaranteed exchangeable to gold. This is seen as the beginning of the era of the Gold Standard.

using it was always the same. (note: the price of gold was much less volatile back then compared to today, partly due to a lack of speculative trading)

During World War I, all Western nations except the United States left the Gold Standard. The US followed in 1933, because of the Great Depression.

BRETTON WOODS

With the end of the second world war approaching, world leaders and economists realized the utmost importance of a quick return to stability in international financial markets. So, in July 1944, one month after D-Day, the allies gathered in the *Mount Washington Hotel* in Bretton Woods, New Hampshire, to discuss the structure of the world economy after the war. The three most important decisions to come out of Bretton Woods, whose influence is still being felt in today's financial world, were:

The founding of the International Monetary Fund (IMF). This organization would oversee the international agreements and support countries in times of an economic crisis with temporary loans if necessary. (the bailouts of Greece, Ireland and Portugal in 2010 and 2011, conceived and funded jointly by the EU and IMF together, show how vital the role of the IMF still is in today's world; in fact, while writing this book, support seems to be growing for an even larger role for the International Monetary Fund as the world's lender of last resort)

The US Dollar would be connected to a fixed gold price of $35 per ounce (It is interesting to compare this to the gold price of $1,920 per troy ounce reached in September 2011). The United States would therefore reintroduce the Gold Standard into its monetary system.

All other currencies would be pegged to the dollar. The currencies of all other countries would therefore automatically be connected to the Gold Standard as well, through their dollar peg. This kind of indirect connectivity is called the *Gold Exchange Standard*. With this system, the US Dollar became the de facto *worldwide reserve currency* (a position it still holds today)

This system worked very well during the first couple of years, until the ever increasing cost of the war in Vietnam forced the United States to leave the Gold Standard in the early 1970s. But even though this effectively ended the Bretton Woods system of creating monetary stability by connecting the most important currency to the Gold Standard, the dollar continued to be the reserve currency, simply because the US economy was by far the most important economy in the world. This showed that, from then on, international monetary stability was pegged to the health of the US dollar. (this is something a growing number of countries – among them the so called BRIC countries, Brazil, Russia, India and China – would like to change, because it forces the rest of the world to sustain the US and finance its debt, regardless of its policies, economic or otherwise)

BIRTH OF THE MODERN CURRENCY MARKET

With the decoupling of the dollar from the Gold Standard in the early 1970s, the era of free floating currencies began. The price of a currency would no longer be fixed to something else – be it gold or the dollar – but solely determined by the free market.

Several initiatives have been undertaken during the past decades to counter some of the more volatile effects of having a free floating currency. One well known example is the use of exchange rate bands, such as the *European Exchange Rate Mechanism*, which was used to stabilize the value of European currencies in preparation for the euro. Another method of stabilizing a currency is fixing its value to that of the US Dollar. As we saw before, several countries used this method under the Bretton Woods accord. Nowadays, it is primarily used by poorer, less stable countries.

Among other countries, China has – off and on – pegged its currency to the dollar during the past two decades. Western countries, particularly the United States, have criticized China for pegging the yuan (a.k.a *renminbi*) to the dollar, because it keeps the yuan artificially cheap, giving China an unfair competitive advantage in exporting its goods.

Fixing currencies has often proved to lead to undesirable economic outcomes over longer periods of time, because it impedes the currency from moving along with changing economic circumstances, increasing the likelihood of things like a real estate bubble and/or an overheated economy – that is, when the fixed currency is too cheap given the growth of the economy.

The man who broke the bank of England

One of the most infamous examples of the undesirable effects of a fixed currency can be found in the 1990s, when a much overvalued British Pound was being challenged by the investor George Soros[4]. The subsequent unfolding of that challenge has given George Soros the – well deserved – nickname 'the man who broke the bank of England'.

At the time, the British Pound was prevented from devaluing too much, because it was trading within the European Exchange Rate Mechanism. However, the real value of the British Pound, given market conditions, was much lower. The Bank of England nevertheless refused to raise the interest rate to increase the Pound's real value, or let the Pound float so it could move freely towards its real

---

4   In 2010, George Soros was placed 35th on Forbes' list of the world's richest people. His estimated net worth is $14,2 billion.

market value.

On Black Wednesday (September 16, 1992) investor George Soros shorted the British Pound with a position in excess of $10 billion. Because of this, the pressure on the British Pound increased so much that nobody dared to buy the Pound anymore. As a result, the British government had no choice but to decide to let the Pound float. Reportedly, Soros made more than 1,1 billion dollar with his short position.

THE FUTURE OF THE FOREX

As I write this, the dollar is still the world's reserve currency. Other currencies, commodities and valuable metals, they are all expressed in terms of value in US Dollars. This means that the United States can still borrow at exceptionally low rates; after all, the failure of the dollar is not an option. Just like there are some banks that are too big to fail – as the financial crisis of 2008 showed – so too are some countries. On top of that list is the United States, keeping the financial world in an iron grip, with the dollar as the dominating, irreplaceable, reserve currency.

But for how long? Over the past ten years, the political and economic world order has profoundly changed. The era of American hegemony – peaking in the second half of the 20th century with an economic boom and victory in the Cold War – seems on its way out with the rise of economic powers like China, India, Brazil and Russia (mentioned before as the BRIC countries, a term coined by Goldman Sachs executive Jim O'Neill[5]).

Thus American free market capitalism is under a new threat, this time not by communism but by *dictatorial capitalism* (in other words: the market is free until the state decide it's not). This was made evident in early 2008, when China said the time had come to think about replacing the dollar as the world's reserve currency. At the time, US Treasury Secretary Timothy Geithner could still whisk that notion away to far, far future land. But one severe economic crisis later and that far away future seems to have come a lot closer.

---

5   O'Neill used the term BRIC for the first time in 2001, in his paper, Building Better Global Economic BRICs.

CHAPTER 2 PRACTICAL INFORMATION ABOUT THE FOREX

WHAT IS THE FOREX EXACTLY

Forex comes from *for-ex*, an acronym of the words *foreign exchange*, also known as the currency market. It is the biggest financial market in the world, with a daily trading volume of about $3,980 billion in 2011. Yet there is no brick and mortar building where all the forex transactions take place and where cocky 23 year old Ferrari owners try to outshout each other in buying and selling dollars and euros. That's because the forex is a so called *Over The Counter* (OTC) market. This means that currency orders aren't being matched on a central exchange but executed by the participants themselves. It's all digital and decentralized, without an overseeing authority.

'The' forex therefore doesn't really exist. It's just a global network of banks, processing electronic currency orders coming from their own dealing rooms, other banks, brokers and multinationals.

OPENING HOURS

Because the forex is a global market without a central exchange or overseeing authority, the market is basically open as long as there are banks to process the currency orders, meaning 24 hours a day, five days a week.

(rock) Around the clock

Using Greenwich Mean Time, the market opens Sunday evening at 22.00 GMT in Sydney, Australia – where it's then 09.00am – followed an hour later by Tokyo, then by Hong Kong, Moscow, Frankfurt and at 09.00 GMT London.

At 14.00 GMT, banks start to open in the United States, starting with New York, then onto Chicago and Denver, all the way to San Francisco. Finally, after they close, the banks in Sydney open again.

The busy hours

Although you can trade currencies 24 hours a day, not every hour is equally busy. The heart of the forex lies in Europe. London for instance, accounts for 23% of the daily, global trading volume, Frankfurt follows at 19%. Together, the European share of the currency pie is therefore about 42%.

During the first two hours after Frankfurt opens (and the rest of the European continent) trading activity is usually elevated. The effects of the financial news that was published between yesterday's close (15.00 and 16.00 GMT respectively for Frankfurt and London) and the morning opening will have to be taken into account, as will be the movements on the forex during the last part of

第六十七　凶

獨自惹開非　豈知身未穏　獨歩上雲岐　枯木未生枝

枯(ぼく)木　未(レ)　生(えだを)　枝

獨(どつ)歩(ぼーて)上　雲(うん)岐(きに)

豈(あに)　知(しらんや)　身(みの)　未(いまだ)　穏

獨(ひとり)自(おのづから)　惹(かん)　開(ひく)　非

○ぐわんもう叶ひがたー　○病人長引　○うせものいでがたー　○まち
人きたらず　○やぶくり、ひきこー見合すべー　○たびだちよろーからず　○
よめとり、むことり、人をか、へるわろー

かれ木になりて、えだはが
生ぜぬなり、いまだといふ
字にてみれば、かれきらは
せぬなり

およばぬのぞみをおこ
ーこころをなやますた
とへなり

わが身ついに、あんお
んたちよぎよよりくーや
身をつーむべー

いまだおだやかならざるを
ー身を
ぜんとして又さわや
ことなり

人ーれず、ひとりと
ぜんとして又さわや
ことなり

浅 草 寺 観 音 籤

第六十七　凶

枯木未生枝

枯れ木になり、枝には葉が生えずに、いまだに春を迎えることのないように、

獨歩上雲岐

かなわぬ望みをおこしても心をますます悩ますだけです。今はその時機ではありません。

豈知身未穏

身のほど知らずに事を起こすと安穏となりません。よく信心し、身を慎みましょう。

獨自惹閑非

前日までの自らの非を悟らないと後に悔やむこととなりましょう。

願望：叶いにくいでしょう。

病気：長引くでしょう。

失物：出にくいでしょう。

待ち人：現れないでしょう。

新築・引越：見合わせた方がよいでしょう。

旅行：良くないでしょう。

結婚・付き合い：悪いでしょう。

No.67　BAD FORTUNE

Weak-ned tree has lost leaves, branches, they have to wait long until go get recovered. Having excessive desire to climb up the ladder to clouds, your mind get confused. At last you may be out of peace and safety, you should be more careful at your way. Stay alone, being unknown to the other people you have to hold problem inside.

*Your request will not be granted. *The patient keeps bed long. *The lost article will not be found. *The person you wait for will not come over. *You had better to stop build a new house and the removal. *You should stop to start a trip. *Marriage of any kind and new employment are both bad.

「浅草寺観音籤」の由来と心得

　御籤の習俗はそのむかし中国より伝えられ、比叡山において、日本独特の吉凶を占う百番の御籤となりました。当初は関西方面で広まりましたが、江戸時代には関東にも広がり、庶民向けに改められて今日の「浅草寺観音籤」となりました。

　観音籤には一番から百番まであり、その吉凶判断には凶・吉・末吉・半吉・小吉・末小吉・大吉の7種類があります。この中、**大吉が出たからといって**油断をしたり、また高慢な態度をとれば、**凶に転じる**こともあります。謙虚で柔和な気持で人々に接するようにしましょう。また凶が出た人も畏（おそれ）ることなく、辛抱強さをもって誠実に過ごすことで、**吉に転じます**。凶の出た人は観音様のご加護を願い、境内の指定場所にこの観音籤を結んで、ご縁つなぎをしてください。

あさくさかんのん　**淺 草 寺**

the US session and the entire Asian session. Traders in the United Kingdom and on the European continent will want to wind down some positions and open or increase others.

Another busy time is between 14.00 and 16.00. At 14.00 GMT New York opens and between 14.00 and 15.00 GMT all three major financial centers for the currency market (London, Frankfurt, New York) are open.

During the Asian session it's often much quieter. Some trading strategies make good use of this, by profiting from the extra boost currency pairs often get when London opens. Another popular trading strategy for the Asian session is scalping, which is a strategy that profits from small, preferably repetitive price movements. We'll talk more about scalping further on, in the strategy section of the book.

WHO IS ACTIVE ON THE FOREX

Up until a few years ago, there were only three active players on the currency market: banks, multinationals and governments. Since then however, a powerful new player has emerged: the individual trader.

The role of the foreign exchange market has changed considerably in the past decades. Though originally the forex existed mostly to ensure smooth sailing for the international monetary system and decrease the currency risk for internationally active businesses, nowadays the biggest trading volume by far (between 70% and 90%) on the forex comes from speculation – trading for profit.

The same goes for other financial markets by the way. This phenomenon arose not only due to the more active role of the individual traders but also through the increasing popularity of proprietary trading among banks. Simply put, banks nowadays trade much more for their own accounts while they used to trade mainly on behalf of customers.

Extra: for banks like Goldman Sachs proprietary trading has been a very lucrative business. However, after the passing of the Dodd-Frank Act[6], banks like GS were forced to (once again) separate their commercial banking activities from their investment banking.

Banks

Banks process their currency orders through their own dealing rooms, via the two main spot market systems, Electronic Broking Services (EBS) and

---

6 Officially known as the Dodd-Frank Wall Street Reform and Consumer Protection Act, it became law on July 21, 2010, and its goal is to reform financial regulation. One result was restricting the maximum leverage brokers based in the US are allowed to offer to 50:1.

Reuters Dealing 3000. The banks process these orders for their customers (multinationals, hedge funds, retail brokers and individual traders) as well as for their own accounts.

Multinationals

Because multinationals operate in different countries, they are exposed to currency risks. For instance, wages and production costs could increase, because the currency of the region where the multinational has established a large part of its production process, is becoming more expensive as compared to other currencies. A local German butcher couldn't care less if the euro appreciates 5% in three months, but a German producer and exporter of chainsaws, who competes in the US with American producers of chain saws, would not be amused when the EUR/USD rises 5% in three months. After all, this would make his chainsaws more expensive for his US customers, unless he slashes his prices (preferably with one of his own chainsaws).

To avoid losses incurred from lower profits and protect themselves against risks like this, multinationals take preventive positions on the forex, something called *hedging*. That German chainsaw producer for instance, could *go long* the euro (buy euro's) in order to compensate for the losses he would have to take on the American market should the euro appreciate. Due to the rising volatility of the currency market, this kind of hedging by multinationals has increased in the past few years.

Governments

Governments have their own reasons for being active on the currency market. Through buying and selling large quantities of their own currency, they can influence the price of the currency as compared to other currencies, which, in turn, could increase the competitiveness of their exports.

The Japanese economy has done this for years, to soften the value of the yen and stimulate the export. As an export-oriented economy, Japan prefers a cheap yen. According to Sony, its profits decline by $68,5 million every time the USD/JPY falls by 1 yen (meaning that you would need less yen to buy 1 dollar). Japanese economists have stated recently however that the Japanese business community should adapt to an appreciating yen, since this situation is likely to continue.

Government action of this sort on the forex is called intervention. Economists agree that even though an intervention can exert great influence on the price of a currency in the short term, the long term effect is very limited. The exponential growth of the forex also makes it ever harder to make a real impact on the market. The volumes needed nowadays to give of a powerful signal to the market, are such that continued intervention has become a very costly thing. On top of that, interventions could also irritate trade partners, triggering a possible currency war, because it artificially increases the competitiveness of a country at the cost of other countries.

Extra: an interesting example is the forex intervention by the Swiss National Bank (SNB) in September 2011; the SNB publicly stated it would from then on defend a minimum of 1,20 Swiss Franc per 1euro with all available means at its disposal. The SNB said it would be willing to buy foreign currencies in "unlimited quantities" to make sure the Swiss Franc would not appreciate beyond 1,20 euro. The reason for this – rather extreme – decision was that in the months before, increasing worries about the European crisis had driven many investors to the Swiss franc, which is considered a 'safe haven' currency. The subsequent rapid appreciation of the franc (16% in a couple of months) was beginning to damage the Swiss economy. After the decision of the SNB, investors started looking for other safe haven currencies, like those in Japan, Brazil, Norway and Sweden, causing the currencies of these countries to appreciate more and as a result damaging their economies.

In rare cases, countries sometimes decide to intervene on the forex together, to put a stop to extreme volatility and instability. One such case was the intervention by the G7 in March 2011, following the earthquake, tsunami and ensuing disaster at the Fukushima nuclear reactors. Forex traders, expecting Japanese companies to repatriate their foreign investments on a large scale, quickly pushed the yen to the highest level in 25 years. Because the G7 countries intervened together, they were able to send a strong signal to the markets that the level of 78 yen for 1 dollar would be vigorously defended. This put an end to the immediate momentum of the USD/JPY bears.

Individual Traders

As previously noted, the individual trader is a relative newcomer to the forex scene. Up until a few years ago, individual traders had no direct access to the forex. The internet – especially broadband internet – has rapidly changed that.

Of course individual traders don't deal directly with the big, international banks. Their access to the forex comes through brokers. You can find a comprehensive list of forex brokers at www.forexforambitiousbeginners.com/forex-brokers.

In the early days, the smallest lot size available to individual traders was the so called *Standard Lot*, which stands for 100,000 units. The maximum leverage was usually 200:1 or lower, meaning you needed at least $500 in trading capital to open just one position. Later, the *Mini Lot* – 10,000 units – was introduced, and many brokers also increased the maximum leverage to 400:1. Nowadays, most brokers also offer Micro Lots, made up of 1,000 units. So a beginning currency trader can now start with a trading capital that is one hundredth of what was needed just a couple of years ago. (note: recent new regulations in the United States have brought down the maximum leverage brokers are allowed to offer their US clients to 50:1. Brokers operating outside the United States have made no changes to the maximum leverage offered to non-US clients)

REGULATIONS

Because the forex is a global, decentralized market, regulations differ according to country. Most countries have financial watchdogs that require brokers and banks that are active in their territory to be regulated by them, but because the foreign exchange is a completely electronic, decentralized spot market, brokers can easily establish themselves in countries or territories where regulation is scarce.

Generally, the bigger brokers let themselves be regulated in countries like the United States, the United Kingdom and the Eurozone, but there are also many brokers that are not – or barely – being regulated (which doesn't necessarily mean they are bad brokers by the way).

The most important regulating authorities overseeing forex brokers are:

- National Futures Association (NFA) – United States
- Securities and Exchange Commission (SEC) – United States
- Financial Services Authority (FSA) – United Kingdom
- Financial Services Agency (FSA) – Japan
- *Bundesanstalt für Finanzdienstleistungsaufsicht (BaFin)* – Germany

CHAPTER 3 HOW CURRENCY RATES ARE DETERMINED

In this chapter we will turn to the foreign exchange market itself for the first time. How are currency rates determined, and how are currencies traded in the first place? For easy illustration it might be a good idea to open an account at a forex broker now (you can do this for free), if you haven't already done so.

See www.forexforambitiousbeginners.com/forex-brokers for a comprehensive list of forex brokers.

The rate of a currency is nothing more than the value of that currency, and that value is always relative. Unlike stocks from a publicly traded company, a currency does not have any real, intrinsic value (at least not anymore; at the time of the Gold Standard – see Chapter 1? when the exchange of currency into gold was guaranteed by the state, it did have real value). The actual value of a currency in daily life – its buying power – can be determined by tracking how much currency is needed to buy a specific selection of goods; this is the method used to measure inflation. But on the forex, we only look at the value of a currency compared to other currencies.

CURRENCY PAIRS

Currencies are traded in pairs. The value of the euro compared to the dollar for instance, is determined by the currency pair EUR/USD (euro/dollar). When the demand for euro's rises, the rate of the EUR/USD will go up. When the demand for euro's falls, the EUR/USD will go down.

Because all currencies are being traded against each other, you can trade in hundreds of different currency pairs at the forex. Not all currency pairs are equally *liquid* however (the more a currency pair is traded, the more liquid it's said to be). The most important, most liquid currency pair is the EUR/USD.

The notation for a currency pair places the abbreviations of the two currencies involved side by side, separated by a slash. Like so: EUR/USD, GBP/USD, USD/JPY , etc.

Currency abbreviations always consist of three letters. The abbreviations for the most important currencies are:
- USD = US Dollar
- EUR = Euro
- JPY = Japanese Yen
- GBP = British Pound
- CHF = Swiss Franc
- CAD = Canadian Dollar
- AUD = Australian Dollar

- NZD = New-Zealand Dollar

The first abbreviation mentioned in a currency pair is called the *base currency*, the second *quote currency*. So when looking at the GBP/USD, the GBP (British Pound) is the base currency, while the USD is the quote currency.

The base currency is the currency you're rooting for when you buy (go long), the quote currency is the currency you're rooting for when you sell (go short) a currency pair. Sticking with the GBP/USD example, when you think the British Pound will go up compared to the US Dollar, you go long the GBP/USD; if you think it will fall, you short the GBP/USD.

By now, you'll have noticed that there is a lot of financial jargon involved when trading the financial markets. Granted, this can be tough when just starting out, but it's important to learn at least some of the most common terminology. You'd have a hard time learning about forex through different sources if you don't understand the meaning of the terms used to describe trading strategies or tactics. It would also make it pretty hard to ask questions to other, more experienced traders. Therefore, in chapter six we will do a crash course in forex terminology. You can also find a short forex dictionary in the back of book for easy reference.

OPENING A POSITION

Buying or selling a currency is called opening a position. Do you think the Euro will go up compared to the US Dollar? Then open a *long* position on the EUR/USD. Think the Euro will fall compared to the British Pound? Open a *short* position on the EUR/GBP.

The image below shows the rates for a couple of currency pairs. If you take a look at the EUR/USD rates, you'll see that there is a difference between the Sell and Buy rate. That difference is called the *spread*. It's what you pay to the broker for opening the position for you. It is important to note that this is also the only fee you'll have to pay your forex broker. There will be no commission, administration costs, subscription costs or any of that, just the spread.

Instrument	Sell	Buy
EUR/USD	1,4023	1,4025
EUR/JPY	108,44	108,49
EUR/CHF	1,2066	1,2070
EUR/GBP	0,8773	0,8778
EUR/CAD	1,3862	1,3870

You can see the spread is very small. At the EUR/USD it's two hundredth of a cent. Forex traders call that a spread of 2 pips[7]. A *pip* is the smallest measured unit of a currency rate. With most currency pairs, this is the fourth number behind the comma. For the Japanese Yen however, it's the second number behind the comma, because the yen is about a 100 times less valuable than the other important currencies)

So when you want to open a short position on the EUR/USD (because you think the euro will decline) you sell the EUR/USD for $1,4023 – using the above example. If you closed the position immediately – without the EUR/USD having moved even one pip – you could do that against a price of $1,4025. Simply put, when you close a short position on the EUR/USD, you do that by *buying* the EUR/USD, thus neutralizing the position you opened. The 2 pip difference goes to the broker.

---

7   Forex brokers differentiate between fixed spreads and floating spreads. Fixed spreads are set in advance while floating spreads can vary, depending on the volatility of the market. Brokers using floating spreads often advertise very low spreads, but beware that they can go up considerably during volatile trading hours.

CHAPTER 4 THE DIFFERENCE BETWEEN FOREX AND STOCKS

The biggest difference between stocks and currencies is in the nature of the product. Owning stock in a company like Royal Dutch Shell will make you part owner of the company (don't go barging into Shell headquarters in The Hague, Netherlands, though, acting like you own the place; even though you do). However, having 10,000 Euro in cash won't give you ownership of anything (other than the cash itself).

NOT AN INVESTMENT MARKET BUT A SPECULATIVE MARKET

A forex position has no intrinsic value, which is why you can't really invest in it. A Standard Lot EUR/USD is worth nothing if the price isn't moving in your direction. But in most cases you *will* be paid dividend when you own Royal Dutch Shell stock and the company has turned a profit (after all, owning stock makes you part owner) -- even when the price of Shell stock hasn't moved at all, or even declined.

Because the value of a currency on the forex is always determined in relation to other currencies, it generally fluctuates more than the value of stocks. The price of a publicly traded, financially healthy company, will normally rise in the long term, because the underlying value of the stock – the company itself – increases over time. In contrast, the price of the EUR/USD will more likely move back and forth than rise in the long term, because the price of this currency pair is not just dependent on the economic health of the Eurozone, but on the economic health of the Eurozone compared to that of the United States, which may very well vary over time.

The candlestick below, of the EUR/USD between 2009 and mid 2011, illustrates this. The price development of the EUR/USD in this period is typically a ranging one, meaning moving sidewards; every trend is only temporary.

EUR/USD
2009 t/m 2011

The forex is therefore much more a speculative market than an investment market. The forex trader makes his money by speculating on the temporary rise or fall of a particular currency. That is not to say there aren't plenty of speculators active on the stock market too, but the core of the stock market players always have been investors, looking for long term investments.

Extra: that it is nevertheless possible to 'invest' in the forex for a longer period of time, has been proven by the investing guru Warren Buffet, who took large long positions on the EUR/USD in 2002, when the rate was pivoting around 0,80. Buffet held that this rate was much too low and did not adequately express the relation between the United States and Europe. When Buffet finally closed down all of his long positions, in August 2008, the EUR/USD had climbed to $1,5950, a rise of 88%.[8]

NOT BASED ON PHYSICAL OWNERSHIP

Another significant difference with the stock market is that a currency trader rarely takes possession of the currency he buys. In that respect, the forex is more like the options- and futures market, which are likewise more about the right / obligation to buy a certain amount of a product at a certain time, then about having that product actually delivered to your backyard. It's therefore no coincidence that forex brokers in the United States are regulated by the *National Futures Association* (NFA)

Physical ownership makes no sense to a currency trader; after all, he can only turn a profit when the rate moves in his direction. There is no dividend, no

8   Reportedly, Buffet's company, Berkshire Hathaway, made $2 billion with this forex bet.

intrinsic increase in the value of the product itself, whereas a company like Shell does increase in value over time, making its stock more valuable as well.

The vast majority of currency positions are closed within 48 hours after they are opened. For most currency traders, the long term isn't all that interesting.

TRADING STOCKS IS MORE EXPENSIVE

Last but not least, two other important differences are that you need much more capital to trade in the stock market, and that small stock traders have to overcome relatively high costs to turn a profit.

Trading stocks with a total capital of $1,000 is almost never worth your while. It would only buy a couple of stocks, and on top of the administrative costs, bank and brokers also charge you for each transaction. Small traders would therefore have to realize 5% ROI (Return On Investment) just to break even.

But $1,000 does give you a real seat at the table on the forex. This is especially true since the introduction of the Micro Lot (where 1 pip is worth about 10 cents) which enables you to open a position for a couple of bucks. And through the use of leverage, you can substantially increase your ROI. (of course leverage can also work against you; more about this later on)

A forex broker charges nothing outside of transaction costs, the spread. No administrative costs, subscription costs, or anything like that. A few brokers charge you for transferring funds to your bank, but the vast majority of brokers only charge spread.

SIMILARITIES

Of course there are also similarities between currencies and stocks. With just a little bit of imagination you could say that a currency is a representation of the economic state of the country that uses it, just like stocks are a function of the economic state of the company that issued them. When Royal Dutch Shell publishes disappointing results and announces it will pay a lower dividend, the price of Shell stock will likely fall. Just as the price of the Euro will likely fall when the growth of the biggest economy in the Eurozone, Germany, falls short of expectations.

Other factors that can influence the value of a currency on the forex are: unemployment figures, consumer confidence, consumer spending, export figures, production figures and producer confidence.

When looking at it like this, the foreign exchange market does resemble the stock market somewhat, and in a way currencies really are a representation of the underlying value of a company of sorts (even if it's not as direct a correlation as with stocks). But keep in mind that even though the price of a currency is influenced – just like the price of a stock – by the underlying value of the economic system it represents, the fundamental difference remains that currencies are paired against each other while stocks are only traded based on their own underlying value. If the stock market ever switches to a system where you can trade in Shell/BP, Toyota/Ford and Apple/Microsoft the stock market and foreign exchange would be much more similar, but the likelihood of this happening is just about equal to that of the United States switching to a Chinese style dictatorial state capitalism.

WHY RECESSIONS DON'T MATTER TO THE FOREX TRADER

Because currencies are traded by pairing them against each other, it doesn't matter for forex trading whether or not a specific economy – or even the entire global economy – is in recession. After all, the fall of one currency in a currency pair would automatically mean the rise of the other currency in that pair.

This is not to say that recessions can't have an impact on the price of a currency – because they can and most definitely do – but they do not really change anything for the currency trader. When the British Pound falls because the United Kingdom has entered a recession, the forex trader sells GBP/USD and goes long the EUR/GBP. Is the Eurozone faring worse than the United Kingdom? No problem, the trader simply shorts the EUR/GBP!

Of course you can go short on the stock market as well (although several governments have limited this practice as of late). Buying *put options* enables traders to speculate on the fall of a specific stock, and the more uncertain the economic times the more stock market traders will revert to shorting the market. But, the longer the time period the more inevitable the upward trend of the stock market also becomes. The reason is simply that publicly traded companies normally turn a profit and grow (when they don't for a longer period of time, they'll eventually disappear from the stock exchange)

The foundation of the stock market is therefore formed by investors holding stocks as an investment; to profit from the yearly paid out dividend and/or the Return On Investment of the stock itself when they sell it off. A recession hurts these investors, because companies will sell less, turn smaller profits or suffer losses, and might even go out of business (rendering the stock worthless).

No Uptick Rule

As mentioned above, the possibility of going short on the stock market is frequently limited by financial authorities, because it is thought that hedge funds et al. would destroy healthy companies in uncertain economic times by shorting them into oblivion. During the first months of the financial crisis of 2008, going short on the stock market was therefore prohibited in several countries (including the United States and Germany, among others) for some time.

Up until 2007, short selling had been limited in the United States through the so called 'uptick rule', which states that one can only go short when the price of a share has risen by at least one tick. This – much derided – rule has since been replaced by the SEC by 'Regulation SHO', regulating what is known as *naked short selling*. However, the SEC reportedly also has the reintroduction of the uptick rule under review.[9]

Thankfully you don't have to worry about these kind of anti-capitalistic rules when trading on the forex. Nobody will raise an eyebrow when you go short on the forex in times of economic distress, because all forex traders regularly short currency pairs, whatever the global economic tide.

---

9   Many economists and politicians have called for the reintroduction of the uptick rule after it was abolished in 2007. Three days after the fall of Lehman Brothers, on September 18, 2008, Senator John McCain – then Republican Presidential candidate – says: "short selling [turns] our markets into a casino."

CHAPTER 5 INDIVIDUAL TRADERS ON THE FOREX

As we have learned, the forex opened up to private traders a relatively short while ago. That has everything to do with the technological revolution set off by the internet, making an array of advanced trading software available to everyone with a common, household computer, enabling them to communicate directly online with the trading terminals of banks and brokers.

Up until fifteen, even ten years ago, the currency market was the exclusive playground of banks, governments and large, institutional players. Big, international banks traded directly with each other through advanced trading systems (as they still do today), while the rest, including smaller banks, bought and sold currencies through those big banks.

ONLINE TRADING PLATFORMS

The big change came when banks and brokers started offering online trading software retail, to individual traders. Thanks to ever faster internet connections and computers, large quantities of online financial data could easily be streamed to the average computer and vice versa, connecting individual traders to the financial markets in real time.

What's most important when choosing a broker is a stable, fast trading platform, that offers ample options to customize your positions. Being able to put in a stop loss and profit target is standard on all trading platforms, but that's not the case for options like *limit orders* (which will only trigger when the currency pair reaches a certain price level) or *trailing stops* (stops that move with your position when the trade moves in your direction).

Many traders also find it increasingly important to have access to the trading platform at all times, be it with a different computer – at home, at work etc – through a web trader, or with a smartphone or tablet. It's therefore advisable to look for a broker that also offers a web version of its software (java based, making it also suitable for Apple computers) as well as mobile apps and tablet apps.

Another important development these past few years has been the surge in freely available technical trading software. Technical analytical indicators could only be calculated manually by traders before the 1980s. Subsequently developed software that automated the task only became available to professional dealing rooms in the years after that. However, in the past decade they've come within easy reach of everybody.

Today, even after opening just a demo account, most forex brokers will offer you sophisticated technical trading instruments that until fairly recently had only been available to well paid professional traders.

A word of advice though: don't lose yourself too much in the use of technical indicators. You really don't need to implement 20 different indicators to come up with a successful trading strategy. Experienced traders will tell you that only a handful of the most well known technical indicators will suffice as tools for a working trading strategy. We'll talk more about this further in the book.

START WITH A SMALL TRADING CAPITAL

In the early days of retail currency trading, the minimum lot size for individual traders was 1 *Standard Lot*, which stands for 100,000 currency units. Using 100:1 leverage – the maximum leverage back then – you needed $1,000 to buy 1 Standard Lot EUR/USD. Even using 400:1 leverage – the current maximum leverage most brokers offer to traders outside the United States – you'd still need $250 to open one Standard Lot position. With 1 pip being about $10 , trading on the forex often remained a proposition too expensive for small, private traders.

That changed when the so called *Mini Lot* was introduced, which is one/tenth of a Standard Lot. 1 pip is worth only $1 in a Mini Lot, and by using 400:1 leverage you only need $25 to open one position.

A while ago, an even smaller lot size was introduced by many brokers, the *Micro Lot*. This – as you probably guessed – is one/hundredth of a Standard Lot, with a pip value of 10 dollar cent.

All this means that when you want to start out small as a forex beginner – which would be the smart thing to do – a couple of hundred dollars will suffice when trading Micro Lots. Because 1 pip is worth only 10 cents with micro lots, you'd command 2,000 pips with a trading capital of just $200.

Chapter 6 Short Forex Lexicon

When being introduced to a subject as big as financial trading, it's easy to get overwhelmed by a barrage of new terms, definitions and concepts. This book is no different in that respect, and unfortunately there is no way around it. Not only would it be highly impractical to keep explaining every term throughout the book, it would also leave you ill prepared for using an online trading platform or reading other books about trading, since they all use the same terminology.

In this chapter we'll have a look at some of the most important terms. This list is also published in the back of the book, to serve as an easy reference whenever you need it. The terms below are used so often over the course of this book, that it is strongly advised to make sure you grasp their meaning before moving on.

Opening a Position

This means buying or selling one or more lots. For example, you can open a position on the forex by buying 1 mini lot EUR/USD.

Long or Short

Whenever you want to speculate that a currency will rise in value, you go long that currency. Conversely, speculating it will fall is called going short (also called *shorting*) the currency.

Stop Loss

This is a predetermined price – somewhere below the break-even point – at which a position will be closed, to prevent further losses. For instance, suppose you buy 1 lot GBP/USD at $1,6250 and place a stop loss at $1,6180, your maximum loss would be 70 pips. In other words, a stop loss enables you to determine, in advance, exactly how much of a loss you're willing to take on a given position. Especially as a beginner, you should **always** put in a stop loss.

Take Profit

A predetermined price – somewhere above the break even point – at which a position will be closed, to take profit. It works the same as a stop loss, only in this case the position is moving in your favor. Many traders put in a take profit (a.k.a a *profit target*) to prevent them from exciting too soon out of fear, or too late, out of greed. Putting in a take profit is not as essential as putting in a stop loss, but beginners would generally do well to use the take profit option, because it trains you to trade according to a predetermined plan – which is one of the most important prerequisites for being successful as a trader.

BULLS & BEARS

Traditionally, the nickname for traders who think the market will go up is *'bulls'*, while those that think the market is going down are called *'bears'*. It's therefore no coincidence that there is a statue of a big, bronze bull[10] on the Wall Street Square in New York City; it symbolizes belief in the *'bullishness of capitalism'*.

BID AND ASK

The broker always offers two rates for a currency pair, the *bid* and *ask*. The bid – always the lowest of the two – is the price for selling or shorting a currency pair. The ask price tells you against what price you can buy the currency pair. The difference between the two rates is called the *spread*.

SPREAD

The difference between the bid and ask price, which is pocketed by the broker for services rendered (namely opening the position for you). So when the bid price for the EUR/USD is 1,4000 and the ask price is 1,4003, the spread is 3 pips.

BASE CURRENCY AND QUOTE CURRENCY

As said, currencies are always traded in pairs. You can trade the euro against the dollar, against the pound, the yen, etc. The currency first mentioned in a currency pair is called the *base currency*. This is the currency that you're de facto buying when you buy a Lot. When you buy one Lot EUR/USD for instance, it means you *go long* the euro. The second currency, in which the base currency is expressed, is called the *quote currency*. For the currency pair EUR/USD, the dollar is therefore the quote currency and the value of the euro is expressed in dollars.

CROSS CURRENCIES

These are currency pairs where the US Dollar as neither base nor quote currency. Examples are the EUR/GBP, EUR/JPY, GBP/JPY. Because these currency pairs are less *liquid* (meaning they are traded less often) their spread is higher.

---

10   The Charging Bull, a.k.a Wall Street Bull, or Bowling Green Bull, is the bronze statue by Arturo Di Modica, weighing 3,200 kilograms. It's seen as a symbol of capitalism and is located in Bowling Green Park, close to Wall Street, Manhattan, New York City.

CANDLESTICK CHART

The most popular way of tracking a currency pair's price development is using a candlestick chart. It consists of 'candles' in two colors (usually red and green), one to signify a period of price rise, the other a period of price decline. The lowest point of the candle shows the lowest price reached during the period, the highest point of the candle shows the highest price reached. A green candle means that the price closed at the high end of the body (thick part) of the candle, a red candle means the price closed at the low end of the body.

Legend has it that the candlestick chart was invented in the seventeenth century by a Japanese rice trader who was looking for a better way to quickly gain insight into the price development of, well, rice.

Volumes have been written about the different patterns that can be discerned from candlestick charts. You will therefore have no trouble getting your fill If you would like to know more about the *Three White Soldiers*, the *Ichumu cloud* and other wonderful chart patterns which sound like they come out of an adult version of Pokémon.[11]

LEVERAGE

Leverage is the ratio between the underlying value of a transaction and the amount of money that is actually being reserved to cover losses. This makes speculating on a financial instrument much easier for traders with only a small trading capital, because they only need a fraction of the total amount of money they are controlling.

Example: using leverage of 400:1 – the maximum leverage at most forex brokers – you would only need $2,50 in available funding to open 1 micro lot EUR/USD.

1 micro lot = 1000 units

leverage 400:1

Available funding needed = 1000/400 = $2,50

Because a pip is 10 cents when buying micro lots, $2,50 will buy you a buffer of 25 pips that the price can move against your position (before it's automatically closed). Put differently, with 400:1 leverage you can control $1000 worth of currency with an investment of only $2,50.

Leverage is a double-edged sword of course, because it magnifies losses as well as profits. It's also what opens up the forex market to smaller traders, who want to trade the financial market more aggressively and thus pursue higher profits.

---

11 According to many, the 'bible' of candlestick chart books is Steve Nilson's Japanese Candlestick Charting Techniques.

STANDARD LOT

A unit of measure that represents 100,000 units of any currency. This original measure has since been joined by the *Mini Lot* (10,000 units) and the *Micro Lot* (1,000 units).

PIP

The smallest measured price change for a currency pair. The fourth number behind the decimal point for most currency pairs (for example, for the EUR/USD: $1.45**22**).

RESISTANCE AND SUPPORT

Price levels a currency pair had trouble breaking in the past or that form a natural barrier, like the psychological $1,5000 level for the EUR/USD

Resistance points are price levels a rising currency pair has trouble breaking. The more often the rally of a currency pair is stopped at a specific resistance level, the stronger that resistance level is said to be.

The same goes for *support*, but in this case with falling prices.

PART II

TRADING ON THE FOREX YOURSELF

CHAPTER 7 YOUR FIRST FOREX ACCOUNT

You learn by doing. With forex trading, that doesn't mean that you should empty your savings account and have at it. On the contrary, the foreign exchange market has little mercy for reckless beginners. On the other hand, you can't learn to swim without getting wet, so you do have to actually trade currencies if you want to become a successful currency trader (if this doesn't make sense to you, now would be the best time to find something less challenging). But nowadays, thanks to micro lots, a couple of hundred dollars will suffice, instead of the couple of thousand (or more) that used to be necessary as minimum trading capital.

Now, even though you can always be that lucky beginner, be aware that opening a GBP/USD position using 400:1 leverage is not the same as buying 100 *Apple* shares. Speculating on the forex while using leverage is fast, dynamic and fluid. It can be highly profitable, but also unprofitable and risky. More experienced forex traders often take advantage of the errors of beginning traders, like placing stop losses and profit targets at obvious price points, or buying into short covering rallies. And because you basically trade against each other on the forex – just like in a poker game – the losers pay the winners. The bank – the casino so to speak – is only a go-between.

Extra: in reality it is more complex, because banks also trade for their own account, something called 'proprietary trading'. However, this is being restricted more and more by governments – especially when accompanied by commercial banking activities. This because the financial crisis of 2008 showed (again) how dangerous it can be when big banks actively trade for their own account with their customers' money.

Is it possible to make it big as a forex trader? Yes, definitely. Smart, talented traders can acquire a small fortune in a relative short time, starting out with a relatively small trading capital. But you won't become one of them by jumping into the deep end green as grass and committing more money than you can afford to lose. So start small and grow big, instead of starting big and ending small.

REQUIRED TRADING CAPITAL

The amount of trading capital you need to trade on the forex depends on your goal(s).

When you're a beginner and just want to try out whether or not currency trading is for you, you won't need more than $200. If you use that to open a micro account with a forex broker, you could trade in micro lot positions of 1,000 units (1pip = 10 dollar cent) and have a buffer of 2,000 pips. That would even be sufficient for conservative money management (more about this later) and more than enough to allow you to trade a while and learn from your mistakes.

If you want to seriously research whether you could live off trading the forex, $200 in trading capital would be enough to test if you have it in you to learn to trade profitably and consistently. A buffer of 2,000 pips at the lowest level would be enough for most strategies to survive the *swings*. (obviously, the smaller your trading capital, the smaller your profits in absolute numbers; So don't expect that $200 to be generating enough cash flow after three months for you to quit your day job).

Many beginning traders lose their first trading capital. There are several reasons for this. For one, finding a trading strategy that suits you takes time and money, as will learning to protect your capital through adequate risk management. And then there are the many psychological pitfalls that come with trading in a fast and exciting financial market. You will have to learn to deal with the frustration of seeing once promising positions tank, sometimes one after the other. You'll have to acquire the discipline needed to put a stop to yourself when your emotional side is telling you to put on *more* risk – to quickly erase earlier losses. Not everybody has what it takes – a calculating, rational personality, especially under fire – to become a successful forex trader.

It is important to realize in advance that learning to become a consistently profitable trader will take time, money and a bit of patience. So don't jump into the deep end right away with money you can't lose, nor should you give up when your first attempt fails and you lose your first $200.

Obviously you can't live off trading the forex with a trading capital of $200. But really, as a beginning trader, it will do you very little good thinking about how much trading capital you'd need to survive as a full time trader. A question that, as it stands, has no easy answer, because it is dependent on a number of factors, such as what trading strategy you use, how much your monthly income should be and how much you'd need in your trading account to make you feel comfortable about your trading buffer.

Therefore, you should first take the time to find out if you can turn a profit at all, over a longer period of time. So start with a trading capital of between $200 – $1,000, trade in small lot sizes and be sure to cover your risk when opening each position (by setting a stop loss) and by giving yourself time to learn from your (inevitable) mistakes.

Choosing the Right Forex Broker

Trading currencies is an active form of speculating. Even traders with a trading horizon of weeks or even months regularly check and tweak their positions, expanding some while winding others down, opening positions on other currency pairs , etc. So you'll probably interact more with the trading platform provided / used by your forex broker than with the online trading facilities you use to invest in stock.

Because you'll likely use it more intensively, the look & feel of the trading platform is important, as is the quality of the customer support offered by the broker. Is there only email / live chat, or also telephone support? 24/5 or 24/7? And how customer friendly are the customer support representatives? These may seem trivial points now, but wait till you have a problem accessing your account, or something went wrong with a withdrawal. These things happen, it's how your broker handles them that makes the difference.

If you use an Apple computer, make sure the trading software the broker offers supports iOS. Even if it doesn't, there are ways around it, but it's much more convenient if the broker also offers a web trader (which is java based).

Another thing to consider is the regulating financial authority. A broker that is regulated by the British FSA or German BaFin instills a little more confidence than one regulated by the financial watchdog of Panama or Mauritius (if regulated at all). An unregulated broker isn't necessarily a bad broker, but it's definitely a plus when the broker is regulated by an independent financial authority of a country with a good reputation in the financial world.

On www.forexforambitiousbeginners.com you can find a comparison of the most important brokers.

DEMO ACCOUNT OR REAL ACCOUNT?

The answer to this question is simple: you need both. There is only one difference between a demo account and a real account: money. The demo account only uses *play money*, whereas the real account is for trading with *real money*.

It's not possible to learn to trade profitably solely through trading on a demo account. That has everything to do with the psychological part of trading. How do you react under pressure, what do you do when the position turns against you when it was so close to the profit target you had put in moments before? Do you close the position right away? And when the price is close to your stop loss? Do you move the stop loss? How do you start your trading day after having been stopped out for three days in a row on more than 70% of your positions, when normally only 30% of your trades are losers?

These are only a few of the situations you will confront as a trader. Situations you will experience very differently when it concerns real money instead of play money. Just as you can't learn to surf on sand, or play poker with matches (unless each match is worth $100) you can't become a successful forex trader by trading for play money either.

Having said that, a demo account can definitely help you get the hang of a new trading platform, or to test out new trading strategies. When testing a new strategy, the fact that you're not trading for real money is a big advantage, because it allows you to test a system under optimum conditions, without any stress clouding your judgement.

OPENING YOUR FIRST POSITION

Ok, provided you have not done so already, let's just open our first position right now. Choose a broker to your liking on www.forexforambitiousbeginners.com/forex-brokers and open a demo account. Or, if you want to start off a little more serious right away, open a real account and deposit something like $200.

Now, suppose you think the price of the euro is going to fall against the dollar. Perhaps there's been some negative news about German employment, after which you looked at the EUR/USD candlestick chart and saw a clear downtrending pattern.

You log into your broker's trading platform, be it from your desktop, through the web trader, or through a mobile app on your smartphone or tablet, you seek out the currency pair EUR/USD and click on 'sell'. Next, you'll have to specify your sell order and that's important, because it allows you to limit your risk and determine a profit target.

The rate of the EUR/USD can easily travel 100 pips in either direction on any given day (remember, a pip is the smallest possible price change, in this case the fourth number behind the comma). Now, because you don't want to get any nasty surprises, you're putting in a stop loss.

At the moment, the EUR/USD is at $1,4215. After studying the candlestick chart earlier, you concluded that should the pair break $1,4250, chances are that it would rise further. You put your stop loss therefore at $1,4260. So should the EUR/USD reach a price of $1,4260, your position would be automatically closed, putting your maximum potential loss at 45 pips. How much money that is, depends on the size of the position.

Because you have no experience yet trading the forex, you decide to open just one micro lot position (1,000 units, 1 pip is 10 dollar cent). Your maximum loss in this case would be 45 x 10 dollar cent + spread of 3 pips = $4,8.

Using 400:1 leverage, you'd need a minimum of $2,5 in your account to open one micro lot position of 1,000 units. The price could then move 25 pips against your position before it would be closed automatically.

However, in this case you elect to give your position a little more breathing room, so you reserve $4,5. The spread, charged by the broker for opening the position, is deducted from your account right away, but profits will only be put into your account when the position is closed.

Since you don't expect the EUR/USD to fall further than $1,4000, you put the profit target at $1,4005. As said, putting in a profit target is not as essential as putting in a stop loss, but it can help you plan your trade, preventing you from getting out too soon; or too late. Beginners are strongly advised to put in a profit target as well as a stop loss. Profit targets and stop losses are not only used by beginners though, many seasoned traders also use them. Apart from acting as a guard against emotional decisions made during the trade, they're also very handy when for some reason (earthquake, internet down, being on a hot date) you can't close the position manually.

You're risking 45 pips to win 210 pips. Even if the trade would only succeed 25% of the time, you'd still turn a nice profit. Watch. You would lose 135 pips (3 x 45) and win 210 pips (1 x 210), for a gross profit of 75 pips. After deducting 4 x 3 pips for the spread, your net profit would come out at 63 pips over 4 trades. Not bad at all.

Satisfied with the way you've set up the trade, you hit 'submit' / 'open' / 'Geronimooooo!' and the position is open. You're now officially a forex trader!

MONEY MANAGEMENT

The importance of money management is often underestimated by forex traders. A lot of time is devoted to searching for and tweaking the ultimate trading strategy, but the question of how best to manage the available trading capital is frequently overlooked. The same goes for the psychology behind trading in the financial markets by the way. We will take a closer look at this later on.

Money management – or rather, the lack thereof – is one of the most important reasons so many beginning traders lose their trading capital faster than they can say *poopty peupty pants*. They become disillusioned and stop trading altogether. Trust me, jumping in the deep end right away, depositing $2,000 and risking $200 per trade will get you no where fast.

Rule number 1: Survive

Whether you're a beginning or experienced trader, your most important mission is to stay in the game (well, your most important mission after making money that is). Losing trades are inevitable, but when you go broke you deprive yourself of the opportunity to offset those losses with profitable trades.

It's therefore important to find out what percentage of your trades is profitable and what your average *risk / reward ratio* is per trade (how many pips do you risk to make x pips in profit). Based on this you'd get an indication of how much you can risk per trade and what your *Expected Value* (EV) per trade is.

Example

Suppose 1 in 4 of your trades is profitable and you have a risk / reward ratio per trade of 1:5, meaning that on average you risk 1 pip to win 5 pips.

Let's also suppose that, on average, you risk 40 pips per position, which, looking at your risk / reward ratio of 1:5, means you stand to gain 200 pips on your winning trades.

Because only 1 in 4 of your trades is profitable, you'll lose 3 x 40 pips, while winning 1 x 200 pips; on average. This would make your gross profit 80 pips over 4 trades. After deducting 4 x 3 pips for the spread your net profit would be 68 pips. Your Expected Value is therefore 68 / 4 = 17 pips per trade.

The good news is that you're trading strategy is EV+. The bad news...well there isn't really any bad news, as long as you realize that the profitability of 1 in 4 trades is just an average; you can easily do much worse over longer periods of time (or better). You should therefore have a healthy buffer in your trading capital.

A good rule of thumb is to have at least 10 times the capital needed to produce one winner. Following the above example, you would need a trading capital sufficient for 40 trades. (because, on average, you need to do 4 trades to produce one winner).

Now, obviously you won't know from the get go how many of your trades will be winners, so the sensible thing to do would be to have enough capital for a minimum of about 40, 50 trades. Supposing each trade would be the size of a micro lot position (1 pip = 10 dollar cent) and needed breathing room of about 50 pips, then one trade would require $5 in capital. (50 pips times 10 cent). So, in order to have enough capital for 50 trades, you'd need 50 x $5 = $250.

Another, frequently used rule of thumb is to never risk more than 2,5% of your capital per trade. You don't have to follow this rule religiously – that would mean you'd have to recalculate after every trade how many pips you can risk – but it's wise to keep it in the back of your head.

We will go deeper into money management later in the book.

WHAT IS A REALISTIC RETURN ON INVESTMENT

The question about a realistic Return On Investment (ROI) for forex trading is frequently asked, but unfortunately it does not have a simple answer. Frequently, the number 35%(for annual ROI) comes up. But although this would not be a bad return on investment at all (the average return on investment on the stock market over a 30 year period is somewhere between 8% – 12% annually) it's completely pulled out of a hat.

Annual ROI – the value an investment yields in a given year – is dependent on a number of factors, among them the chosen trading strategy, how much risk is involved per trade and the frequency with which an initial investment is reinvested.

For instance, a trend trader with a starting capital of $250, who opens about ten positions per year of one micro lot each, and gains 500 pips per year, or a profit of $50, realizes a Return On Investment of 20% with his $250 initial investment. Should he double the frequency of his trades, he could also double his ROI. Obviously it's not always quite as simple as this to improve one's ROI, but sometimes all a trader lacks is time to trade more often. Something else to take into account is that not every strategy is suitable for every trader, nor does every trader have the same *risk appetite*, even if it would mean a (much) higher return on investment.

A scalper who executes 100 trades per day and earns an average 0,5 pips per trade, would need 100 trades to make the same amount of pips as the above mentioned trend trader. But because the scalper is much more active with his trading capital – executing 100 trades per day instead of 10 per year – he can easily reach a much, much higher ROI annually over his initial investment.

But when you're just starting out as a forex trader it's really more meaningful to focus on your Expected Value (EV) per trade and making sure it's positive (by closely monitoring your risk / reward ratio) instead of blindly focussing on your possible annual ROI. That comes later.

Later, when you're consistently profitable on the forex, you can try and find out whether or not the ROI you're getting from your trading strategy favorably compares to what other, consistently profitable traders are earning with the same trading strategy.

AUTOMATED TRADING YES OR NO?

When talking about automated trading, we should distinguish between two different forms:

1. Building your own *Expert Advisor* (a.k.a Forex Bot)

2. Buying an existing *Expert Advisor*

Your Own Expert Advisor

Every trading strategy can be automated, although some are easier to define in solid parameters than others. If you have a little aptitude for programming, you could consider building your own expert advisor / forex bot.[12]

The idea is to program the conditions that have to be met to trigger the trade into your expert advisor (EA), after which the EA will take positions for you whenever those conditions are met. Or, when you don't want a fully automated system (fearing your awesome programming powers might bring about a world ruled by robots) you could set the EA up to simply warn you when the set-up is triggered.

Working with your own expert advisor can have several important advantages. One is that it will take emotion out of the equation; after all, positions will be triggered only when certain, rationally pre-defined conditions have been met. Another is that it clears the way for a much more analytical approach of your trading strategy, making it easier to tweak it going forward. Lastly, using an expert advisor would enable you to take advantage of (many) more trading opportunities, because the EA would monitor the markets for you, either alerting you when a currency pair meets the pre-defined conditions, or opening a position outright in such cases.

There is software available that can help you to build an EA, but as pointed out, some aptitude for programming is required.

Buying an Existing Expert Advisor / Forex Bot

Getting an EA that promises to work *out of the box* usually has only limited value. Since you didn't build the FX bot yourself, you will have no feeling for the underlying parameters that define the set-up, which increases the chance that the trading strategy isn't right for you.

Where it is possible to change the parameters of the EA you could perhaps tweak it enough to turn it into a profitable trading strategy, but then again, when the EA is based on faulty premisses, you can tweak all you want but you will never get a consistently profitable trading system.

The most interesting option for expert advisors therefore remains building one yourself (or having it built by a qualified person) based on the parameters of a set-up that has proven itself to you.

---

12   By building an expert advisor for the MetaTrader 4 trading platform for instance, using the MT programming language, MQL4.

5 TIPS THAT WILL SAVE YOU MONEY

The 5 tips listed below are mentioned throughout this book. That's because even though they can't guarantee success – nothing ever can, otherwise everybody would be successful – they *can* save you a lot of money. Experience shows that many beginning forex traders bleed money mainly because they fail to follow the next five principles:

1. Money Management

Rule number 1 for every forex trader is to survive. Every trader has losing trades, but when you go broke you put yourself in a position where you can no longer have winning trades. Therefore, before everything else you have to make sure you stay in the game. Many beginning and / or consistently losing traders focus exclusively on having a profitable trading strategy. But even though a good trading strategy is definitely important, using solid money management and having a rational, disciplined trading attitude will get you further at the end of the day. Two rules of thumb for good money management are not to risk more than 2,5% of your trading capital per trade and making sure you have enough trading capital for at least 40 trades when you are a beginner.

2. Always Use a Stop Loss

The stop loss is perhaps the most powerful weapon in your arsenal as a forex trader, just as the most powerful weapon of the professional poker player is the *fold* (if that means anything to you). The stop loss allows you to predetermine your risk down to the pip, therefore ALWAYS use it!

There are really only advantages to putting in a stop loss. It forces you to think about when the trade you're about to put on would be considered a failure. After you've opened the position you might talk yourself into staying in a trade going bad, using all kinds of irrational excuses. But if you've set a stop loss before opening the trade (when you were still thinking rationally) you'll always have that shining beacon, reminding you that you'd be a weak, emotional idiot if you stayed in the trade after the stop loss is triggered.

Setting a stop loss also forces you to think about your profitable trades / losing trades ratio. Suppose you want to risk 50 pips to win 100 pips, that would mean you'd need a winning trade at least 33% of the time to break even. Does your trading strategy get you a profitable trade 33% of the time?

Another advantage of the stop loss is that you don't have to be afraid that one badly chosen trade will kill your whole account in case the trade goes bad and for some reason you're not in a position to close it manually. So remember to always put in a stop loss and never move it further away after opening the trade.

3. Be Realistic

Unless you are amazingly lucky you can't expect to close 80% of your trades profitably or turn a $500 trading capital into a $10,000 trading capital in six months. A normal human being with those kind of expectations you're simply setting yourself up for disappointment, frustration and failure. (unless you're very, very lucky). Try to look at things realistically right from the start. Determine an attainable percentage of winning trades considering your strategy and experience. Ask yourself how much time you can spend on trading and learning. When you have a clear view of your trading tools and conditions, you will find it much easier to work towards a profitable trading strategy.

For example, suppose you're a day trader with a trading strategy where you risk, on average, 15 pips to win 30. After doing about 200 trades, it turns out that 50% of your trades reached their profit target of 30 pips; the other 50% of the trades went sour and triggered your stop loss. So you've won 100 x 30 pips = 3,000 pips and lost 100 x 15 pips = 1,500 pips, for a gross revenue of 1.500 pips total. Gross revenue, because you still have to deduct the spread, i.e. the transaction cost you pay your broker, remember? Let's say the spread is 2 pips per position, meaning your 200 trades costed you 400 pips. Your net revenue then, was 1.100 pips over 200 trades, or 5.5 pips per trade.

Of course data on 200 trades isn't enough yet to be of statistical significance, but at least it would give you something to work with: on average, each trade nets you 5,5 pips.

4. Interact with Other Traders

For beginning traders an often overlooked source of information is other traders. Of course, reading books about forex is important. Books can provide you with a solid basis in a short time, providing a foundation to build on. Practicing is another important factor to get the hang of things quickly, but you'd be surprised to find out how often fellow traders can give you valuable feedback about your trading strategy, or about alternative ways for putting on a particular trade. You should therefore become part of an online forex community and consider starting a trading blog, so people can comment on your strategy. Don't be embarrassed because you're a beginner; remember that we all started out as beginners at some point, and many of the traders you'll meet on online trading forums are also just starting out.

5. Keep Your Emotions under Control

This last tip is perhaps the most important one. As previously said, trading on the forex is exciting, fun and dynamic, but it's crucial not to get carried away because of this. Successful traders approach trading like a business, not a hobby.

Forex for Ambitious Beginners - 55

You use your trading capital to make business decisions; some will make you money, others will cost money, it's that simple. But as soon as you lose sight of your rationality I promise you that the losses will stack up pretty quickly.

I'm talking about those moments that you do move your stop loss, because you just can't get yourself to take the hit. Or those moments that you decide to get in right now, even though your trading plan tells you to wait, because you're so scared to miss the trade, or perhaps you're just bored. Those moments that you're so mad that you lost 10 trades in a row that you start trading with triple your normal risk, taking positions in currency pairs you normally never trade in.

Those are the moments you lose in 30 minutes what it took you three weeks to build up.

PART III

UNDERSTANDING AND PREDICTING PRICE MOVEMENTS

CHAPTER 8 THE FOUR MOST IMPORTANT CURRENCIES ON THE FOREX – AND THE YUAN

WHAT MAKES THE US DOLLAR SO IMPORTANT

The most important currency by far on the forex is the US Dollar. The US economy is also still by far the largest in the world[13], all commodities are priced and traded in dollars, and the USD is either base or quote currency in the five most important currency pairs (EUR/USD, GBP/USD, USD/JPY, USD/CHF, USD/CAD)

The dollar's current, globally dominant position is still (partly) based on the *Bretton Woods* accords of 1944, where it was decided that the Gold Standard would be reinstated for the US Dollar and that all other currencies would be connected to the US Dollar. This marked the beginning of the American dollar as the world's *reserve currency*, causing all countries to keep large amounts of reserves in both gold and US Dollars.

This made the dollar the *de facto* foundation of the international monetary system, a coveted position the dollar holds to this day, even though the core of Bretton Woods – reinstating the Gold Standard for the US Dollar and pegging the other currencies to the dollar, thus stabilizing the international monetary system – ceased to exist in the 1970s, when the United States had to leave the Gold Standard due to the high cost of the Vietnam War.

Because the dollar is the global reserve currency, countries keep large reserves in dollars in the form of US Treasury bonds. The United States' largest creditor is China, which possessed more than $1,1 trillion in US Treasury bonds in 2011.[14] Although the US national debt has substantially increased in the first decade of the twenty-first century, borrowing rates for the US remain relatively low, because US T-Bonds are generally in demand and the risk of a US default is deemed extremely unlikely. (However, the United States lost its triple A rating at rating agency Standard & Poor's in august 2011; the reason, according to S&P's, was because political parties remained unable to come to an agreement on how to bring down the public deficit)

The Federal Reserve

Monetary policy in the United States is decided and carried out by the Federal Reserve, the Fed. The most important job of the Fed is stimulating economic growth and guarding price stability. Although the Federal Reserve is an

13   The GDP of the United States was $14,657 billion in 2010. China's was $5,878 billion. The GDP of the EU was higher, at $16,282 billion, but although it is seen as one economic region, it is not the same as a country.

14   http://www.treasury.gov/resource-center/data-chart-center/tic/Documents/mfh.txt

independent institution, the appointment of its chairman is a political affair. The President appoints a candidate, who subsequently has to be confirmed by Congress.

Extra: Due to the sharp rise in unemployment, caused by the financial crisis of 2008, the chairman of the Federal Reserve, Ben S. Bernanke, mentioned another task of the Federal Reserve in 2010, namely stimulating full employment. At that time, US unemployment was above 9,5%. To stimulate investment – which would create jobs – the Fed therefore decided to pump a $600 billion stimulus into the economy by buying US Treasury Bonds. A practice known as quantitative easing – because it increases the money supply. The rate of the dollar fell considerably lower because of this.

Another instrument the Fed has at its disposal to influence the dollar is the ability to change the interest it charges other banks for borrowing money from it. This so called *discount rate* was lowered to close to 0% by the Federal Reserve during the financial crisis of 2008. By contrast, the European Central Bank (ECB) only lowered the rate to 1% during the same period.

WHERE IS THE CHINESE YUAN?

The currency of the second largest economy in the world, the Chinese Yuan – a.k.a. *renminbi* – is still not a free floating currency. The value of the yuan is determined by the Chinese central bank, the People's Bank of China (PBOC).The Chinese government is keeping a tight grip on its economy and manipulation of its own currency is certainly a part of that. This is despite the fact that it is becoming clear, slowly but certainly, that the omnipresent Chinese government cannot completely control the forces of the free market the Chinese economy is now a part of.

Up until a few years ago, the value of the Yuan was simply pegged to the dollar by the PBOC. The robust growth of the Chinese economy was therefore barely reflected by the Yuan, because it could not appreciate freely and was instead linked to the growth of the American economy. So even though the Chinese economy was booming and demand for the yuan rose accordingly – because of the booming economy – its value was kept artificially low, much to the chagrin of the United States and Europe, since the cheap yuan also artificially improved the competitiveness of Chinese exports (at the cost of the U.S and Europe).

Extra: in 2005 China 'depegged' the yuan from the dollar, causing the currency to appreciate immediately. During the financial crisis of 2008-2009 the POBC put the dollar peg back on, only to depeg again in June 2010. An IMF staff paper written in 2010 stated that the yuan was undervalued between 5 to 27 percent.

Still, even China acknowledges the need for the yuan to develop towards a freely tradable currency. In the first place to counter rising inflation, caused by a combination of a fast growing economy and an artificially low currency.[15] Since the cheap yuan is keeping the value of goods and services artificially low, prices push ever higher. A yuan valued more realistically would have a dampening effect on inflation.

In the second place, China would like to get rid of US dominance in the global monetary system, which allows the United States to borrow at rock bottom rates. Due to the dollar's role as reserve currency, the fate of the global economy is also deeply connected to the fate of the dollar, and thus of the United States. That means that China is, in effect, obliged to help keep the United States afloat.

In recent years, China has voiced a preference for a global monetary system based on the IMF's (artificial) weighed currency, called *Special Drawing Rights* (SDR) instead of the US Dollar. The SDR is a weighed average of the world's most important currencies, including the US Dollar, the Euro, the British Pound and the Japanese Yen. It is not a currency but can represent claims to currencies. It is the unit of account for the IMF. Some think SDR's might have an important future role to play as the world's reserve currency.

Though China's proposition has been met with cautious approval by several countries, most also point out that before the SDR could be used as a global reserve currency, the Chinese Yuan should also figure into the weighed average. For that to happen, the yuan would have to be floated and become a freely tradable currency.

China has already taken some (baby) steps toward this goal – albeit on a limited scale – notably by experimenting with a freely tradable yuan in Hong Kong. Economists expect the yuan to become freely tradable on the forex in the not so distant future.

THE EURO

The euro, the youngest of the world's six most important currencies, was introduced as an electronic currency in 1999 and is the most important currency on the forex after the US Dollar. It is the shared currency of the European Monetary Union (EMU), minus the United Kingdom, Sweden and Denmark. The European countries that share the euro, seventeen in all, are: Germany, France, Italy, Spain, the Netherlands, Belgium, Austria, Greece, Ireland, Finland, Portugal, Malta, Cyprus, Estonia, Slovenia, Slovakia and Luxembourg.

The European Monetary Union is the world's largest economic block, boasting a (combined) GDP of 16,820 billion euros in 2010. Stock, bond- and future markets

---

15   The IMF estimated in 2010 that the yuan was between 5 and 27 percent undervalued.

in Europe have been relatively stable over the past decades, making those markets attractive for investors worldwide. This, in turn, drives the demand for the euro. (These past few years have not been quite so stable of course. However, provided the eurozone can put its debt crisis behind it, European financial markets will in all likelihood return to pre-crisis levels of stability).

The EMU is responsible for about 20% of global export and 18% of global import. As a whole, the EMU has a modest trade surplus.

The euro had a somewhat rocky start, diving down towards $0,80 from its introductory price of $1,20 in the first months of its existence. However, in the following years, the rate of the euro rose above $1,60, more than double its low point. Even during the eurozone's darkest hours in 2011 – when the very survival of the euro and the eurozone as a whole was regularly called into question – the euro never fell below its introduction price of $1,20.

Extra: According to several economists, the financial crisis of 2008 and the subsequent European debt crisis that started in 2009, brought the eurozone to the brink of a breakup, and the common currency to the brink of destruction. The admission by Greece, in 2009, that it had lied for years about the true scale of its public debt and yearly budget deficit, not only triggered a debt crisis in Greece and other weaker euro countries (a.k.a PIIGS, for Portugal, Ireland, Italy, Greece and Spain) but also uncovered a fundamental weakness of the European Monetary Union: sharing a currency without sharing an underlying fiscal- and political unity.

European Central Bank

Though the eurozone countries lack fiscal and budgetary unity – the most important reason for the European debt crisis according to most economists – they do have a common monetary policy, enforced by the European Central Bank (ECB).

The ECB is the independent central bank of the European Monetary Union, charged with guarding price stability of the euro. At the heart of guarding price stability is the ECB's policy on inflation. When inflation in the Eurozone rises and stays above 2 percent for a longer period of time, the ECB will intervene, in the first place by raising the interest rate it charges national central banks and normal banks for borrowing. How long 'too long' is, will be determined by the ECB on a case by case basis.

The interest rate is set once a month at a policy meeting. After the meeting, the decision is published and explained by the President of the ECB, during his monthly press conference. The press conference (broadcasted live on the ECB's website) other remarks the President makes – and to a lesser extent, remarks made by other members of the ECB's governing board – are all carefully monitored by forex traders who are looking for hints about policy decisions that could have a profound effect on the euro, both in the short and long term.

EUR/USD

The currency pair EUR/USD is the most liquid currency pair on the forex. The EUR/JPY and EUR/GBP are the most liquid *currency crosses*. For beginning forex traders the EUR/USD can be a great pair to start with, because its movements are often somewhat more predictable than those of the other important currency pairs (a.k.a *the Majors*), which is partly due to the high liquidity of the pair. Traders living in the eurozone might get an added advantage from having more *feel* for the euro itself as well as for the most important economies of the eurozone.

Things You Should Know about the EUR/USD

As with every currency pair, the value of the euro vs. the dollar is a function of the economic relations between two macro-economic entities, in this case the 17 countries that make up the Eurozone, and the United States. Figures about the US economy and that of the EU therefore have a direct impact on the price movements of the EUR/USD.

There are also geo-political factors at play, perhaps more so than with most other currency pairs. US and European foreign policy developments, internal power struggles and the cooperation within the EU block (or lack thereof) it can all be of influence on the EUR/USD.

Important Economic Indicators for the Euro Are:

- **US and Eurozone Preliminary GDP**. The economic growth of both the US and the Eurozone is an important factor for the EUR/USD, because price movement for the pair in essence illustrates the health of the two economies relative to each other.
- **German unemployment figures**. Making up about 30% of the total Eurozone GDP, Germany is by far its largest economy.[16] Since the unemployment figures are an important gauge for the health of the economy as a whole, German unemployment figures are nothing to sneeze at when it comes to the health of Europe.
- **Non-Farm Payrolls**. These are the US employment figures minus government and agricultural jobs. As the US economy is the largest in the world, its employment figures can have an impact on virtually all currency pairs.

---

16   The German GDP was $3,315 billion in 2010, followed by France with a GDP of $2,582 billion and Italy with a GDP of $2,055 billion.

- **German and US production figures**. Production figures are an important gauge for the health of an economy, and as such can have an impact on the EUR/USD.
- **Consumer Price Index** (CPI). This is the inflation figure. Both the European Central Bank and the Federal Reserve look at this figure to determine whether or not measures have to be taken to reign in inflation.

Trading Opportunities for the EUR/USD

The EUR/USD has a trading range of about 100 pips during the European trading session (from 08.00 GMT to 16.00 GMT). This is approximately the same as the trading range of the USD/JPY, but substantially less than the 150 – 200 pip range of the GBP/USD. This implies that the EUR/USD is less volatile than the GBP/USD (a.k.a. the *Cable*; a nickname originating from the time when GBP/USD quotes between New York and London were synchronized through a communications cable under the Atlantic Ocean), which is indeed the case. Because of its greater volatility, the spread (difference between bid and ask) that brokers charge for the Cable is almost always higher than the one for the EUR/USD.

The EUR/USD generally moves in reasonably reliable and easily identifiable patterns, making it a good candidate for intra-day range trading (meaning capitalizing on sideward movements during the day). The first two hours of the European session tend to be volatile and the direction for the pair during those hours often runs contrary to the rest of the day. During the Asian trading session the EUR/USD is usually very calm, moving in tight ranges, which makes it a good candidate for a scalping strategy (you can find more on scalping in chapter 17).

THE JAPANESE YEN

The Japanese economy is the third largest economy in the world – after the United States and China (or the fourth largest, if you count the Eurozone as one economy) – with a GDP of $5,400 billion in 2010. Japan is known as an export economy; 15% of its GDP is contributed by its export sector.

During the 1970s and 1980s, the Japanese economy grew at a rapid clip, similar to the growth of the Chinese economy in the first decade of the twenty-first century. The rapid expansion rate caused the Japanese economy to overheat, provoking fast rising prices and an asset bubble. When that bubble collapsed in the early 1990s, it resulted in a banking crisis and the beginning of a massive national debt build up.

In many ways, Japan still hasn't overcome its financial crisis of the 1990s. The banking sector is still relatively weak and the national debt has continued to increase over the past decade. In 2011, it totaled 229% of GDP. This is by far the highest public debt level of all the industrialized nations. By comparison, the public debt level of the United States seems almost modest at 103% of GDP.

Ministry of Finance and the Bank of Japan

The Bank of Japan's (BOJ) primary responsibility as central bank is controlling the monetary policy of Japan. Although the BOJ is in many ways independent of the Ministry of Finance (MOF), this particular ministry still has a lot of influence when it comes to Japan's monetary- and foreign exchange policy. Therefore, comments from both the BOJ and the MOF are important when it comes to predicting price movements of the yen.

The stagnation of the Japanese economy that followed the banking crisis of the 1990s has led to a policy of extreme monetary easing by the Bank of Japan. This is because a cheap yen is important to the Japanese export sector – and the export sector is an important part of the Japanese economy. As a result, the BOJ and the Ministry of Finance pursue a policy of active intervention on the forex, to prevent the yen from appreciating too much. The interest rate the BOJ charges other banks also has been extremely low for years – close to 0% – making money extremely cheap for Japanese banks.

Important Economic Indicators for the Yen:
- **GDP**. The economic growth figures give a strong indication of the health of the economy. The impact on the forex comes primarily from the preliminary GDP figures, because they're the first confirmation (or denial) of other, secondary economic signals.
- **Industrial production**. Production figures generally give a good indication of the state of the economy. For Japan, the amount of industrial output is particular important, as its economy is for a large part dependent on international trade.
- **Employment**. The more people that are working, the better it is for the economy. It is not only good for domestic consumption but also a strong sign that business is good. The employment figures are published monthly by the Japanese *Bureau of Management and Coordination.*

USD/JPY

The dollar yen – or USD/JPY – is the most liquid currency pair of the forex after the EUR/USD and the GBP/USD. Because the Japanese central bank frequently tries to influence the price of the yen by intervening on the forex (or threatening to do so), the USD/JPY is one of the more volatile currency pairs.

The value of the yen as compared to the dollar is expressed as an X amount of Japanese Yen against 1 US Dollar. Therefore, when the rate of the dollar/yen is 91,81, this means that 1 dollar is worth 91,81 yen at that moment.

Extra: The rate of the USD/JPY reached a high point in 2002, when it hit 1,3515, but has since fallen dramatically. After the earthquake and tsunami of 2011, the USD/JPY fell to 76.25, the strongest level for the yen against the dollar since the end of World War II. This situation resulted from currency traders suspecting that Japanese companies and investors would repatriate considerable foreign funds, as is usual in Japan in times of crisis. Joint intervention by the Japanese central bank and other important central banks, prevented the yen from falling even further.

What Should You Pay Attention to When Trading the USD/JPY

The yen is often used as a vehicle for the carry trade. With this trading strategy, a currency with a low interest rate is traded against a currency that carries a high interest rate – in order to profit from the difference in interest between the two assets. (more about the carry trade in chapter 20). Because the interest rate for the Japanese Yen has been close to 0% for years – and is also highly unlikely to change in the medium term – the yen is deemed an ideal low interest rate currency for the carry trade.

The popularity of the carry trade increases when traditionally high interest rate currencies are poised to increase their interest rates further,for instance to cool off their economy and/or to battle inflation. When the carry trade rises in popularity, downward pressure on the yen increases, because in a carry trade the yen will be sold against a higher yielding currency. In a worsening economic climate, however, the opposite is true; many carry trades will be closed (or stopped out) because high interest rate countries lower their interest rates, to stimulate their economy. So in times of economic distress, the chance increases that the yen will rise.

Currency pairs the Japanese Yen is a part of – including the USD/JPY – become more active towards the end of the Japanese fiscal year (March 31). This is due to certain Japanese laws that require companies that do business overseas to *repatriate* (exchange for domestic currency) foreign earnings during this period. This causes the demand for the yen to (temporarily) surge. Forex traders increase the impact of this practice by speculating pro yen, so as to profit from the effect of the repatriations.

THE BRITISH POUND

The British economy is the sixth largest economy in the world, with a GDP of $2,247 billion in 2010. The United Kingdom opted out of participating in the euro, as did Sweden and Denmark. For the British, saying 'Cheerio' to their beloved Pound was simply a bridge too far at the time. Of course there is always a chance that the British will adopt the euro at a later time of course. But the problems that began to surround the euro from 2009 on – with the advent of the Greek credit crisis – have diminished what little enthusiasm there was left for the common currency to something resembling an after party without beer. (of course, when it comes to schadenfreude, quite the opposite is the case)

Bank of England

The British central bank, or Bank of England (BOE) is independent of the government and is responsible for Britain's monetary policy. Its primary job is guarding the price stability of the British Pound. The BOE aims for an inflation rate between 0,5 and 2 percent.

GBP/USD

The GBP/USD is one of the most liquid currency pairs on the forex. Approximately 14 percent of all currency trades are in the GBP/USD. That makes it the second most traded currency pair, after the EUR/USD.

The value of the pound compared to the US dollar is expressed as 1 British Pound for an X amount of dollars. If the GBP/USD is at 1,40 for instance, it means that 1 British Pound equals $1,4.

The pound dollar is often called the *Cable* by traders, a term that comes from the time when the rate of the GBP/USD in New York and London was matched by exchanging telegrams between the two cities.

What Influences the Cable

The rate of the GBP/USD is primarily influenced by the economic circumstances in the United States and Great Britain. Important economic data from both countries can therefore have a direct impact on the rate of the pound dollar.

Examples of important economic data that impact the Cable are:
- **Interest rate decision Federal Reserve** (FED)
- **Interest rate decision Bank of England** (BOE)
- **British employment figures**
- **US employment figures** (non-farm payrolls)
- **British Gross Domestic Product** (GDP)
- **US Gross Domestic Product**

The GBP/USD in Relation to Other Currency Pairs

The GBP/USD has a positive correlation with the EUR/USD and a *negative* correlation with the USD/CHF (US Dollar / Swiss Franc) meaning it often moves in the opposite direction from the USD/CHF. This is because the three European currencies mentioned – British Pound, Euro, Swiss Franc – are correlated positively with each other, through the important economic ties between these economic regions.

Trading Opportunities for the GBP/USD

The GBP/USD is one of the most volatile currency pairs on the forex and therefore not the easiest pair to trade. Price movements of the GBP/USD are characterized by an abundance of false breakouts (more on false breakouts in chapter 19) and random swings that can prove costly to novice traders. For the more experienced day trader however, the Cable offers regular chances for a quick profit, augmented by the relatively wide range of the pair.

The daily range of the GBP/USD lies between 150 and 200 pips. Looking at it from the profit end, this means you could pocket 150 pips profit on an average day when you're on the right end of the move, while potential losses can be limited beforehand, to 20, 30 pips per trade. Deploying a successful trading strategy for the Cable generally requires a large buffer though, because of the higher risk that trades will be stopped out on account of the volatility of the pair. Therefore, again, not a very suitable currency pair for beginning forex traders.

The best time to trade the pound dollar is during the European session, when both Frankfurt and London are open for business. The pair is the most liquid during that period. Of course some trading strategies (and/or trading personalities) require a quieter time to trade the GBP/USD; during the Asian session for instance, the then usually very tight trading range of the Cable is ideal for many forex scalpers (the trading strategy scalping is discussed in chapter 17).

CHAPTER 10 FUNDAMENTAL ANALYSIS

Fundamental analysis takes into account all the forces that influence the economy, such as production capacity, consumer confidence, employment data, etc. Fundamental analysis can help explain past price movements and predict future ones.

While financial news is very important to the fundamental analyst, it's important to realize that fundamental analysis is more than just following and understanding financial news. The fundamental analyst isn't necessarily guided by the news of the day, but is instead trying to draw conclusions about a currency's direction in the medium to long term. Subsequently, he opens positions on the market (partly) based on these conclusions.

Fundamental analysis matters to almost all traders – even if trading based on technical analysis is preferred by most traders nowadays. The reason for the continued importance of fundamental analysis is that the value of every currency is based on the economic circumstances in the region using the currency. Changes in those economic circumstances impact that value. As a currency trader you should therefore take those (changing) economic circumstances into account.

One of the challenges of fundamental analysis is the fact that it doesn't really include market sentiment. Someone using a trading strategy based solely on fundamental analysis will therefore regularly feel that the price is moving in the wrong direction, given the underlying economic data.

However, a technical day trader that doesn't take publications of economic data into account will also find himself stopped out often. Prices of currency pairs can become highly volatile right before and after important economic figures are published and technical indicators cannot predict these kind of swings.

Thus the most successful forex traders use both fundamental and technical analysis. To highly successful billionaire trader Bruce Kovner had something very pertinent to say about this. When asked whether he deemed technical or fundamental analysis more useful, he replied: "This is like asking a doctor whether he would prefer treating a patient with diagnostics or with a chart monitoring his condition. You need both."[17]

WHY ECONOMIC NEWS IS IMPORTANT

Economic indicators give all kinds of hints about the state of a nation's economy and the needs of both foreign and domestic companies operating

[17] Bruce Kovner, a hedge fund manager with an estimated net worth of $4,5 billion in 2011, in an interview with Jack D. Schwager, for his book Market Wizards.

in that economy. Has the central bank of a country lowered its interest rate? That means it will be cheaper to borrow money and also to invest. The money market will expand, generally causing the currency to weaken compared to other currencies.

Governments and multinational corporations 'create' the financial news. This news has both real and speculative value. The real value is determined by the actions and reactions of companies and governments, the speculative value is determined by traders.

Forex Traders Big and Small React to Financial News Because:

It says something about how multinationals (as well as smaller companies) have operated over the preceding period and how they are likely **going** to operate in the coming period. They might decrease economic activity in a particular country for instance, and therefore have less need to hedge against price movements in the currency of that country. *Example*: has the GDP of a country gone up markedly compared to other countries? Then the currency of that country will probably go up in demand. After all, companies like to invest in a country that is doing well. The value of the currency compared to other currencies will therefore probably go up.

It says something about the likely, future behavior of the government who's country the news was about. *Example*: has the inflation within the Eurozone increased to 5%? Chances are that the European Central Bank, the ECB, will increase the interest rate, tightening the money market, (hopefully) causing inflation to decline. The value of the euro will likely go up in this case.

Other traders big and small will **also** react to this news. Perhaps this is the most important reason why traders react to financial news: the expectation other traders will also react to it.

FUNDAMENTAL ANALYSIS AT WORK

The currency market is dynamic and transparent. News often has a direct impact on rates. Real news, but also – and at least as important – speculative news.

As one age old adage from the financial markets goes: *Buy on the rumor, sell on the news*. It means that the rumor about a specific future event is often enough to drive the price up or down. This is so much so the case in fact, that by the time the event itself takes place, it's often already priced in – meaning the effect of the event, positive or negative, has already been added to the price. Often, the real event can even cause a counter move, because of profit taking and/or expectations that weren't matched.

The effect of remarks made by leading board members of important central banks like the ECB, the FED and the BOE is a well known example of this. Every word the chairman of the Federal Reserve (the American central bank) utters, is picked apart and analyzed. The chairman knows this of course, and will therefore choose his words very carefully. Over the years, a whole dictionary of special words and phrases has come about, enabling the chairman to send out signals without saying much. For instance, when the Fed chairman says that *"inflationary indicators point towards a more protracted, higher level of inflation than previously thought"*, chances are that the American central bank will soon raise the interest rate. In anticipation of the official decision to raise the rate, traders will start increasing their long positions on the dollar, causing it to rise, so that the interest rate increase is priced in long before the Fed announces the actual decision to raise the rate.

Therefore, when you expect a currency pair to react to the publication of a certain economic event, first try to determine if that reaction hasn't already taken place, based on rumors about the upcoming event. On the other hand, when a fresh rumor presents itself and you think it's reliable, it could certainly pay off to open a position based on that rumor. When more and more traders pick up on the rumor and put on similar positions, the trade will move in your desired direction. This will enable you to close the position before the rumor ever becomes news, and to pocket a nice profit.

It's important to think about what positions you want to put on and why. Are there several websites predicting a temporary rally of the US dollar? Is the media speculating about important macro-economic data coming from Japan? Is the ECB poised to come out with an interest rate decision? It might seem tough in the beginning to keep track of all that information, but after a while you'll develop an acute sense and be able to evaluate the importance and possible impact of different news events on the forex, allowing you to use this information to your advantage in trading.

Simply put, fundamental analysis at work means getting information from different, reliable sources, distilling the direction of the currency pair based on that information, studying a candlestick chart to see how the currency pair has been doing and subsequently putting on a position (don't forget to limit your risk in advance).

Let's look at an example. On the homepage of fxnews247.com you read the headline: 'Euro under pressure because of rumor no more German support for Greece'. Read the article and determine if the rumor is supported by arguments. Next, check other financial news media like Bloomberg or Reuters to see if they corroborate the story. If they do, it's time to take a look at the (candlestick) charts of the EUR/USD, choosing time frames that match your strategy (for instance, if you're a day trader you won't have much use for a weeklychart, but should instead look at daily, hourly and 15 mincharts). If you see a decline in the rate of the EUR/USD during the past couple of days, does it look to be part of an established downtrend, or did it start to decline only after negative news about the Greek crisis started coming through again, following weeks of relative peace and quiet? And how has the EUR/USD been moving over the past hours? If it looks like the pair is reacting to the rumor, it might be smart to put on a position and ride the wave.

Always make sure you put a stop loss in place, limiting your losses when the movement of the pair in your direction turns out to be short lived.

Once you've decided on a good stop loss and profit target for your position, it's important to stick to your guns. Don't start doubting yourself after you've put on the trade. You set up the trade to the best of your abilities, so have a little faith in yourself. Many traders accrue more losses than necessary by moving their stop loss when it looks like they're going to be stopped out, hoping the trade will still turn in their favor eventually (unfortunately, hope rarely gets you anywhere as a trader). Or they close their position too soon, before hitting their profit target, thus limiting their profits, out of fear the trade will turn for the worse. Don't fall prey to these irrational hopes and fears, remain steadfast in your trades.

THE FOUR FUNDAMENTAL THEMES INFLUENCING THE FOREX

There are four fundamental themes driving the currency market:
1. Economic growth
2. Interest rates
3. Trade balance
4. Political stability

Economic Growth

The strength of a currency is first and foremost determined by the strength of the economy in which it functions. And just as quarterly and annual reports of a company tell you a lot about the economic health of that company, so does economic information put out by a country tell you a lot about the economic health of that country.

Important data about economic growth:

Gross Domestic Product (GDP). Usually published a month after the quarter ends, these are in effect quarterly growth reports.

Employment data. Most developed countries publish employment figures, but the most important employment data is the so called *non farm payrolls*, which are the employment figures for the U.S economy, published by the *Bureau of*

Labor Statistics. These reports show how many jobs were gained or lost in the US economy, excluding jobs in the agricultural sector and government.

Consumer spending. In many economies domestic consumption forms the largest sector of the economy. In the United States for instance, 70% of the GDP is made up of domestic consumption.

Consumer confidence. When citizens no longer have faith in their economic future, they'll spend less and save more, in anticipation of hard times. Lower consumer confidence therefore translates directly into lower consumption.

Production figures. When companies produce more, they hire more workers and will invest more often in new machines, which in turn gives more work to companies producing those machines, causing them to hire more workers , etc. Put simply, higher production figures mean higher economic growth.

Interest Rates

Anybody that took high school economics knows that economies are subject to cyclical trends, rising and falling over time. The highs and lows of those trends change more often in the short term than in the long term (say 50 years).

In light of this, two of the most important tasks of the state when it comes to macro-economics are to stimulate GDP growth and to contain the cyclical movements of the economy in order to prevent excessive highs and lows.

The first point makes sense. The more Gross Domestic Product grows, the richer the country and the more prosperous its citizens (well, most of the time anyway)

The second point makes just as much sense, but perhaps this is not immediately evident. Obviously, cyclical lows should be countered, nobody likes recessions and depressions, but what's wrong with a high flying economy, with companies that are on fire, jobs for everybody and then some? Well, that has to do with the old saying *what goes up, must come down*. A booming economy is great, but if left unchecked it will lead to an overheated economy, with real estate bubbles, high inflation, rising wages, a tighter labor market and an ever expanding money market, because everybody wants to invest in that hot economy.

Until....The Big Turn Around.[18] The market sentiment changes, companies suffer from a huge overproduction, people have to be laid off, applications for unemployment benefits rise through the roof, government expenses rise while tax revenues fall (thus creating huge budget deficits) the money market

---

18   The overheating of the Japanese economy in the second half of the 1980s is an example of this. It was followed by the crash of the Tokyo Stock Exchange at the beginning of the 1990s and the bursting of the real estate bubble that had been forming. In the following years, the Japanese economy grew by only 1,5% a year. The period between1990 and 2000 is known in Japan as the Lost Decade.

tightens, investments fall and the economy takes a nose dive.

Since nobody wants a situation like that, governments generally try to rein in the excesses of the economy's cyclical movements by aiming for lower highs and higher lows. One important part of this is maintaining price stability. Traditionally, this is the job of a country's central bank. A central bank can, among other things, increase or decrease the available capital by adjusting the interest rate it charges commercial banks. For instance, when it becomes more expensive for commercial banks to borrow money, it will also become more expensive for companies to borrow money from banks to invest; the economy will therefore likely cool off. Conversely, when borrowing money becomes cheaper, an economy will likely attract more investments.

Remember: when the interest rate is raised, the money market tightens – because it becomes more expensive to borrow – and the value of the currency rises. When the interest rate is lowered, the money market expands and the value of the currency generally decreases.

Central bank policy has been one of the most important factors driving the forex these past few years. Examples abound – some of them infamous – of central banks trying to influence the currency market by lowering the interest rate or by directly intervening on the forex itself through the buying or selling of currencies. The Bank of Japan (BOJ) in particular is known for intervening on the forex, taking on huge positions to influence (read: lower) the rate of the yen.

Two interest rate increases by the European Central Bank, in mid 2011, constitute another noteworthy example of central bank policy influencing the forex. The EUR/USD rose 700 pips after then ECB President Jean-Claude Trichet gave of a first hint that he would raise the rates if inflation remained above 2 percent. Upon coming into office a couple of months later, Trichet's successor, Mario Draghi, immediately cut the interest rate again, back to what they had been. Many economists agreed with Draghi, believing Trichet had focussed too much on inflation, thereby neglecting the quickly deteriorating state of the European economy, which needed more liquidity (meaning cheaper money, and thus lower interest rates) to rebound.

Mind, that it's not just the actual rate decision of the Federal Reserve, Bank of England, Bank of Japan or ECB that counts, but also the remarks from central bank board members, especially chairmans / governors / presidents. Their speeches and press conferences are closely watched for clues about future policy decisions. That doesn't mean you have to put the microphone in the face of the chairman of the Federal Reserve yourself, or listen to every speech word for word, but be sure to keep an eye on the financial news media about noteworthy remarks from central bank members.

Trade Balance

Suppose the United States imports 100 billion dollars more goods more from the Eurozone than it exports. To import those goods the Americans need euros. So in effect, they will buy 100 billion dollars worth of euros. The US trade deficit therefore causes the euro to rise in value compared to the dollar.

Of course the reality is more complex than the above example (what to think of US companies that export goods from within the eurozone to the United States for example?). However, it is important to understand that the value of a currency can decline when the trade balance deteriorates.

Therefore, when it turns out that the US trade balance fell by 3% after it was forecasted to decline only by 2%, there is a good chance the US dollar will decline in value.

Political Stability

The FX is influenced by politics much more than stock markets are. This is understandable, because on the forex one basically trades in national economies, not in individual companies. Political instability of a nation can harm economic growth in that nation and thus weaken its currency.

Think about the euro crisis; at least part of the euro's decline in value was caused by the continuous bickering of European leaders as to how best solve the credit crisis that first engulfed Greece, Ireland and Portugal, followed by Italy and Spain, and finally the whole of the Eurozone.

Note

Even though you might see more value in technical trading (which we'll talk about next) it would still be smart to keep an eye on these four fundamental themes. Data about employment, economic growth, important developments in national legislatures/politics (for instance, the dispute in the US Congress over raising the national debt ceiling, in 2011, causing concern on the financial markets) and interest rate decisions, they can all have a direct impact on a currency pair, no matter what technical indicators say.

Chapter 11 Technical Analysis

Technical analysis is the study of past price movements, with the objective of predicting future price movements. Many of the most successful trading strategies are based on technical analysis.

Aside from price charts, technical analysts also use what are called *technical indicators*. These are mathematical formulas that zoom in on a specific aspect of the price development, for instance a specific current price of a currency compared to the average price over the past 100 periods.

In the old days, technical indicators were calculated manually by traders and were known only to professionals in the business. Now, they are readily and cheaply available to the millions of amateurs trading on the forex over high-speed internet. They are even included in the free trading platforms provided by forex brokers. Due to these factors, the importance of technical indicators has increased significantly. However, because many more traders are using technical indicators, sometimes following them blindly, technical signals have also become something of a self-fulfilling prophecy.

So it's important to realize that, at the end of the day, currency prices aren't made by news updates, technical indicators or even government policy; they are formed through the actions and reactions of the participators on the forex. Realizing this is half the war.

Charting and Judging Price Developments

Technical analysts study price developments from the past and try to predict future price movements based on that. This is possible because even though there are what can be incomprehensible, and (seemingly) random periods in every price development, it is, for the most part, made up of recognizable patterns.

Some of these patterns can be found by simply plotting daily closing prices on an x-y axis. If, for instance, you plotted each daily close of the EUR/USD this way (of course the forex doesn't really close during the week, so you'd simply pick a fixed time each day) and looked at the development of the pair over the course of a couple of months, you'd certainly see recurring patterns. But before you start plotting prices enthusiastically yourself, you could of course also simply look at an automatically generated chart on your broker's trading platform and study the development of the EUR/USD without having to do any of the dirty work yourself.

Take a look at the forex chart below, which shows the price development of the EUR/USD between 2006 and June 2008 (every candle represents one month).

You don't have to be Sherlock Holmes to find a rising trend here ("this is *really* elementary, Watson"). Since typically there aren't that many trend reversals in the long term, it would have made sense in 2007 and 2008 to simply follow that trend by opening a long position on the EUR/USD (i.e., buying euro's and selling dollars). Of course this is a simplification of the price development of a currency pair, but it does illustrate how you can get valuable information about a currency pair simply by looking at its chart.

EUR/USD 2006 - 2008

DIFFERENT WAYS OF LOOKING AT PRICE DEVELOPMENTS

There are roughly three ways to consider price developments

1. The development of the price over time
2. The development of the development of the price over time
3. The development of the price in different time frames

The Development of the Price over Time

This is simply the plotting of prices during a specific period.

The Development of the Development of the Price over Time

Many of the best, most popular technical indicators are so called 'derivative' indicators: they look at the development of the development of the price. An important reason for their popularity is that they easily filter out 'fake' (or, more accurately, short-lived) developments and therefore give a clearer view of what's going on in the market.

The Development of the Price in Different Time Frames

How the price of a currency pair developed during the past 60 minutes can be an entirely different story from how it developed during the past 24 hours, or 30 days. Technical analysts therefore tend to look at different time frames, depending on their trading horizon (intra-day, daily, weekly etc). So an intra-day trader might choose to look at 15 minute, 4 hour and daily charts, to get a feel for the development of the price and be better able to pick the right entry and exit point for his trade.

CANDLESTICK CHARTS

Technical analysis and candlestick charts go together like peanut butter & jelly, like Laurel & Hardy, peas & carrots, Spock & Kirk, well, you get the idea. Even though most brokers offer the option of showing currency pairs on line charts and bar charts, the vast majority of traders only use candlesticks. The simple truth is that they offer more information, and in a clearer format than either a line chart or a bar chart.

Even though the candlestick chart is the most popular way of plotting prices, it's far from new. The candlestick chart was invented by Japanese rice traders in the Seventeenth century (or at least so goes the legend). The great thing about the candlestick chart is that it shows almost perfectly what happened with the price of a currency pair during a certain period. What the highest price was, the lowest price, the closing price, how far the price traveled, and whether the price was in the middle of a rally when it closed, or just after momentum had dissipated. Because the candlestick uses two different colors – one for falling prices and one for rising prices – you can also see how the price developed over the course of several periods.

There are all sorts of candles and candle patterns, like the *doji* candle, the *long-legged doji* candle, the *gravestone doji*, the *harami*, the *hammer, dark cloud cover, three black crows, three white soldiers*, etc. If you want to dig deeper into the world of candlestick patterns, I suggest picking up Greg Morris' book[19] *Candlestick Charting Explained*.

Some Examples of Candlesticks and Candlestick Patterns

The Doji

This is a candle without a body The doji shows there was indecisiveness in the market. There was some price movement, as shown by the so called *shadows*, the extremities that show the highest and lowest price during the period the candle stands for, but the closing price is about the same as the opening price. So therefore not a lot of price action occurred.

---

19   Another well known book about candlestick charts is Steve Nilson's Japanese Candlestick Charting Techniques.

Three White Soldiers

The nickname for three green candles in a row. It means there is a strong uptrend and chances are it will continue. A good rule of thumb is that the longer a trend is in place, the bigger the chance it will remain so. Naturally, this isn't written in stone, just keep it in the back of your mind when looking at a trend.

The Hammer

This is a candle with a small body and a large shadow. It's a bullish reversal pattern when it shows up in a downtrend – meaning chances are that the trend is about to change direction. The reason is simple: the price was falling, but somewhere during the period of this candle the price started moving in the opposite direction. Apparently, the low price was unsustainable, causing the price to rise. At the end of the period, almost the entire price decline was neutralized.

Conversely, when this candle is shown during an uptrend, it means there is an increased chance of a declining price in the near future; such a pattern is called the *hanging man*.

The *inverted hammer* is a hammer turned on its head, following a series of red candles. The implication is that the price – after falling for several periods – is trying to rise during the period of the inverted hammer, but can't seem to muster enough strength for it yet. There is a good chance the price will try to rise again in the next period.

CHAPTER 12 CHART PATTERNS

Technical and fundamental traders agree on at least one thing: price developments are not completely random. Because if they were, neither following the news, nor studying charts or using technical indicators would make any sense.

Being a technical trader, you can nowadays let the technical indicators do all the work when it comes to predicting future price movements, but most successful traders have learned to recognize certain patterns in the charts for themselves.

By studying forex charts yourself, you will not only get more of a feeling for the normal price development of a specific currency pair, but will also develop a much more profound understanding of it. Like Cipher tells Neo in *The Matrix*, as strains of green code run down the screen: *"I don't even see the code anymore, all I see is blonde, brunette, redhead."*

One look at a random forex chart is good for a treasure trove of information. For instance, take a look at the candlestick chart of the EUR/USD from December 2009 to March 2010 (each candle is 1 week). It won't cost you a lot of effort to see that the rate of the EUR/USD fell considerably during the first months of 2010. The chart won't tell you *why* it happened of course, but it does give a pretty good picture of how it did.

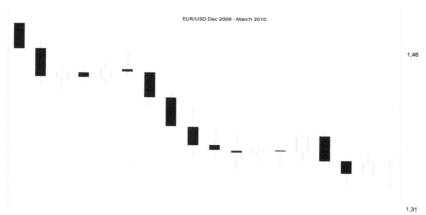

The movement of currency pair is caused by human action. Traders, hedge funds, multinationals, governments and banks all put on positions on the forex and the sum of those positions determines which way the rate of the currency pair goes. And while human actions are partly ambivalent, emotional and exaggerated, they are not random. In the long term, human actions on the forex are rational, because everybody is trying to make or save money through their positions on the currency market.

If the price development of a currency pair is not random, it means there must be patterns; patterns that are, in essence, nothing more than the translation of human behavior into prices on a chart. A classic example of such a pattern is the *double top/double bottom*. With a double top pattern, the price first reaches a new high, then falls back. Somewhat later, it rises to the same high but fails again to move higher still, after which the price collapses. The explanation for this pattern is that the buyers (a.k.a the *bulls*) lose interest in the product, thus creating a sellers (or *bear*) market.

HEAD-AND-SHOULDERS

This pattern is often the harbinger of a nice, profitable trade. It's usually clearly visible and regarded as a reliable signal. The head-and-shoulders pattern is known as a *reversal pattern*, because it's often a sign that the current trend is ending and price development will head in the other direction.

The head-and-shoulders pattern consists of four parts: two shoulders, a head and a neck line. The pattern is said to be confirmed when the neck line is broken. Traders spotting a head-and-shoulders pattern generally plot their entry order just below the neck line, once the pattern is confirmed.

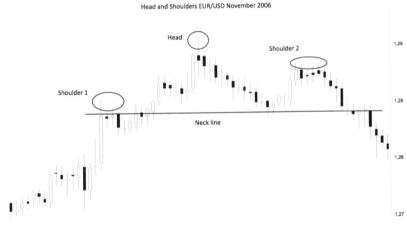

Head and Shoulders EUR/USD November 2006

You don't need much imagination to view the head-and-shoulders pattern as the graphic illustration of a temporary climax in the everlasting battle between the bulls and the bears. First, the bulls, the buyers, reach a new high (first *shoulder*). Unfortunately for them, they are unable to hold on to the peak, and the price falls back again. After some time, they make another attempt and reach an even higher peak (the head).

But the price sags again, until it reaches the *neck line* (the horizontal line in the chart). Again the bulls push the price up, but this time, it doesn't reach beyond the first peak (second *shoulder*). This is a sign of major weakness, since it shows that the new push packs less of a punch than the last one.

There's also such a thing as the reverse head-and-shoulder pattern. See the chart below for an illustration of this pattern.

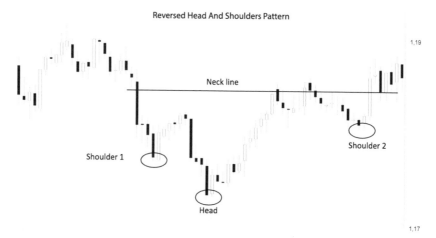

Reversed Head And Shoulders Pattern

DOUBLE TOP / DOUBLE BOTTOM

This is another easily recognizable pattern. In the case of the double top, the price tries to continue in an upwarding trend. But after having failed twice, the bulls lose heart and the price sags like a failed soufflé. The same goes for the double bottom pattern, only this time the other way around.

The first phase of the double top is for the price to reach a new high. However, this high turns out to be too tough to crack, and the price falls back.

During the second phase, the price rises again, aiming once more for the high it had to abandon before. But, just like last time, it does not break through and the price falls again. Keep in mind that the price doesn't necessarily have to hit the high, as long as it comes close.

The second failure is much more serious than the first one, because it confirms earlier indications that this particular resistance might be hard to breach. (a general rule of thumb holds that resistance and support – i.e. the highs and lows – become stronger with every attack they withstand).

It's important not to get in the trade too quickly when spotting a double top/ double bottom pattern. Open the position only after the price has actually broken the support level. You want to hold back because it is possible that the price will start ranging between support and top for a while, before the actual breakout takes place.

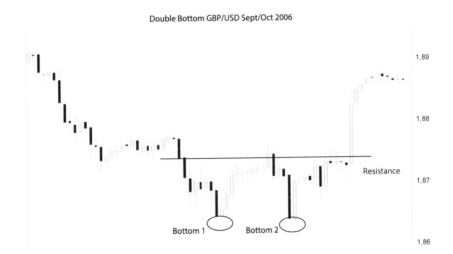

Double Bottom GBP/USD Sept/Oct 2006

TRIANGLE PATTERN

This is one of the most interesting patterns. There are basically three kinds of triangle patterns:

1. Symmetrical triangle
2. Rising triangle
3. Falling triangle

Symmetrical Triangle

When a symmetrical triangle forms, neither the bulls nor the bears can really get a controlling grip on the market. The result is falling highs and rising lows, causing the price movement to narrow.

Have a look at the next chart. The market is continuously making lower highs and higher lows. The highs and lows are drawing ever closer to each other, until there's hardly any variation in price. Such a symmetrical triangle (a.k.a *flag pattern*) can often lead to a profitable trade, when the price breaks out of the flag pattern, be it upwards or downwards.

USD/CAD april 2011

In such a situation, no trader can predict in which direction the price is going to breakout, but that doesn't matter. The goal is to get in once the breakout has started, whatever the direction.

The best trading strategy in a situation like this is to place two *entry orders* (an order that's triggered only when the price reaches a certain level): one placed just above the falling resistance line and one just below the rising support line. This way you'll have a good chance to ride the wave of the breakout, whatever direction it's taking.

Stops should be placed reasonably tight with trades like this, for instance just within the triangle itself. Because when the price moves back within the triangle quickly, the entry signal simply proved to be false.

Rising Triangle

In the case of a rising triangle, the price makes ever higher lows, but is not able to pierce a specific resistance on the other side. This pattern looks a bit like the double top pattern, only without a clear support level at the bottom end. The bears are clearly losing strength, because the lowest price level continues to rise, but the bulls aren't able to take full advantage of the situation.

With a rising triangle, a breakout takes place on the upside more often than on the downside. (bear in mind though that more often doesn't mean always; breakouts to the downside do happen with rising triangles). As with the symmetrical triangle, place an entry order both above the resistance line as well as well as below the rising support line. This way the direction of the breakout doesn't matter. (you can set your stops pretty tight here as well, to limit possible losses)

The most important signal for the rising triangle is the rising support line, because this is what's showing the bears are losing the battle. When the sellers lose heart altogether, the buyers (the bulls) take over and push the price beyond the resistance level.

A rising triangle is often preceded by an upward trend, but can also come from a falling trend.

Falling Triangle

The opposite of a rising triangle (if you hadn't thought of it yet) is of course the falling triangle. The highs go lower and lower, while the price doesn't quite succeed in breaking a specific support level on the other side. The differences between highs and lows become smaller and smaller, until either the bears or the bulls – in case of the falling triangle usually the bears – have gained enough momentum to push the price through the support or resistance level.

Descending Triangle EUR/USD December 2010

A much used set-up for the falling triangle is – as with the symmetrical and rising triangle – to place two entry orders, one above the falling resistance line and one above the support line.

CHAPTER 13 SUPPORT AND RESISTANCE

The concept of support and resistance is one of the most important tools you can use as a trader. These are price levels where supply and demand concentrate, **in the opposite direction of the prevailing trend of that moment.**

Say there is a falling trend – put another way, a period when there is more seller volume than buyer volume – until the price reaches a point where a lot of buyer volume is concentrated, clustered as it were. Suddenly, buyer volume outweighs seller volume – apparently many traders think the price has now reached a point where it's cheap enough to get in – and the falling trend is stopped. See the next chart for an example; the vertical lines represent the buyers volume at a given price point.

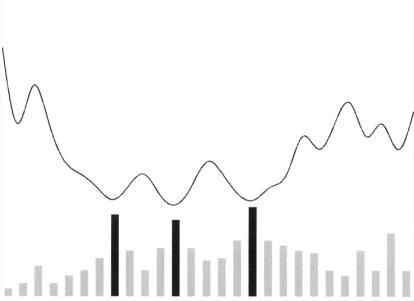

There are support and resistance levels for every time frame – 5 minute charts (1 candle for every 5 minutes), 15 minute charts, 30 minutes, 1 hour, daily, etc – but the longer the time frame, the more entrenched the corresponding support and resistance levels. This makes sense, since it is more significant when a currency pair has broken a certain level only once in the past 5 years, instead of only once in the past 5 minutes.

A support / resistance level has generally withstood at least one attack – otherwise it wouldn't be called support/resistance. (there are also untested, psychologically significant levels, but without having been tested, they can't really be called support/resistance yet, even though chances are that a price movement would run out of steam upon reaching them). Because the support/resistance point has already fended off an attack once, there is a good chance it will succeed at this again. All traders have the same charts in front of them and the collective memory of the trading community is strong.

When a specific resistance level is seen as tough to break, the chance increases that traders close down their positions and take profit when the price approaches this level. Part of the strength of support/resistance points is therefore caused by self fulfilling prophecy.

The more often a support / resistance level withstands an attack, the stronger that level becomes. Knowing these levels – which can easily be spotted on candlestick charts – can bring you important strategic advantages as a forex trader.

CAUSES OF SUPPORT AND RESISTANCE LEVELS

There are several possible reasons why clusters of buyers/sellers volumes form at certain points. Often they are simply psychologically significant levels. One famous example comes from the Dow Jones stock market and the resistance at 1,000 points. Between 1966 and 1982, that 1,000 points resistance proved unbreakable for traders. It was touched a couple of times, but no durable break was made. After such a break was finally made in 1982, the 2,000, 3,000, 4,000, 5,000 levels were pierced relatively easily. Another example is the gold price, that didn't go above $400 from the mid 1980s till the first part of the 1990s.

HOW TO USE SUPPORT AND RESISTANCE

Support and resistance can be a great tool for determining entries and exits for your positions. Armed with nothing but a candlestick chart, you could spot support and resistance points and determine the best strategy to take advantage of them, without using even one technical indicator.

One of the side effects of technical indicators becoming widely and freely available, is that some of the more novice traders hardly really look at candlestick charts themselves anymore, other than to see what this or that technical indicator looks like on the chart. But the truth is that you don't need a technical indicator to spot a good trend, nor do you need TI's to see where the price could not maintain a trend.

As a trader, you can profit from support and resistance levels by treating them as hints about future price developments. A good moment to open a position for example, is when the price bounces back from a support/resistance level. After such a bounce, chances are that the price won't break through any time soon. Place your stop a little above/below the point the price reached, and your profit target a little before the support/resistance on the other side. The next chart may help illustrate this point.

As noted before, there are support and resistance levels for all time frames, but the bigger the time frame, the more important support and resistance become.

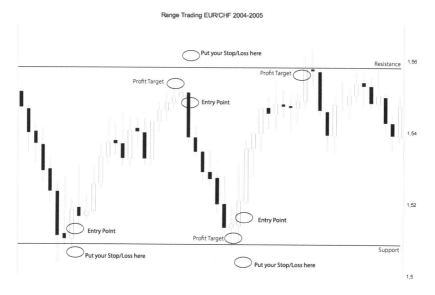

Within the span of one trading session, Intra-day support/resistance levels can be found. These could be price points that determine the trading range for that day, because day traders decide to sell or buy beyond that level. Support and resistance levels within trading sessions can be tens or even more than 100 pips apart, as is often the case with the GBP/USD during the European session. Alternatively, the range can sometimes be only a few pips, which is routinely seen in the EUR/GBP during the Asian trading session.

SOME TIPS FOR USING SUPPORT AND RESISTANCE

Some of these tips have been mentioned before, but it can't hurt to walk through them once again.

1. The faster the price moved before hitting the support/resistance roadblock, the more significant that particular roadblock. This makes sense, since a sudden standstill is more telling than a price that's moving down, down... slower....slower......still slower....stop.

2. The more often a support/resistance has withstood an attack, the stronger it becomes. This is the most important hint you'll get about the importance of a specific resistance/support. When a support has held out three times already, you and millions of other traders know that there is a significant chance it will happen again. This generates great trading opportunities.

3. The larger the timeframe of the chart where the resistance/support can be spotted, the more important that resistance/support probably is. As said before, there are also support and resistance levels on a 5 minute chart. These are less significant than those on larger timeframes though – unless the same levels are also visible on charts with larger timeframes of course. That doesn't mean they can't be of use (or very profitable). When you're an intra-day trader and keep positions open for a maximum of two hours, with profit targets of about 30 pips, support and resistance levels on a 5 minute chart can be extremely useful to you.

4. The more time that has gone by between the first and the last time a support/resistance level has been attacked, the less significant that level becomes. Time is somewhat relative here, because the significance diminishes much faster on a 5 minute chart than on a weekly one. The idea here is that the more time has elapsed since traders actually traded close to those support/resistance levels, the less important those levels become.

Don't make spotting support and resistance levels too complicated. If you are unable to spot them without all kinds of aides and tools on the primary chart for your set-up, odds are that they won't have much of an impact anyway.

CHAPTER 14 THE MOST IMPORTANT TECHNICAL INDICATORS

Technical indicators (also called *technicals*, or *TI's* for short) are mathematical formulas, based on specific parameters, that focus on aspects of past price movements of a financial instrument (i.e. currency pairs in forex trading) and use the resulting information to make a prediction about future price movements.

In other words: a technical indicator looks at price developments in the past and based on that makes it easier to predict future price movements. A technical indicator (TI) does not look at the underlying fundamentals of a stock or financial instrument – like employment data or inflation figures – it only looks at price development. This makes TI's primarily interesting for short term traders, because fundamental factors have a significant impact on price development of stocks and financial instruments in the long term. That's not to say that a long term trader won't still use technical indicators to determine his entry and exit points – just that they are likely to be more accurate in the short term.

There are many technical indicators and it goes beyond the scope of this book to cover them all, but some of the most important ones deserve some extra attention.

MOVING AVERAGES

The simplest way to say something meaningful about a price level is to look at its relative value, compared to other, earlier price levels. This can be done by calculating the *Simple Moving Average*, or SMA, of a price development.

The SMA is the result of the sum of the closing prices of a tradable instrument (in this case currency pairs), divided by the number of closing prices. For instance, to get a 10-period SMA you'd add the closing prices of 10 periods and divide that sum by 10. For every new closing price you add, you remove the oldest closing price. Plotting this 10-period SMA on an x-y axis would show the development of the average price for a given tradable instrument, during the last 10 periods.

The weak point of the SMA is that its *lag*, the distance from the reality of the moment, is rather big. Important SMA's, like the 100 SMA and the 200 SMA (looking at 100 and 200 periods respectively) take price levels into account from a long time ago. At the same time though, these SMA's paint a reasonably accurate picture of market consensus. They give you an idea of where the current price level is, relative to the long(er) term trend. If prices are above the SMA, they are said to be in an uptrend, if they are below it, they're in a downtrend. Simple, yes, but SMA's nevertheless have there uses.

SMA Derivative Indicators, Methods

Several of the more accurate technical indicators are based on the idea of the SMA, such as the Exponential Moving Average and the 3 SMA filter.

Exponential Moving Average (EMA)

The *Exponential Moving Average* (EMA) works the same way as the SMA, only it gives greater importance to more recent price levels. The idea behind this is obvious: the more recent the price, the more relevant it is when looking at the (near) future. An example of an EMA calculation would be to multiply the most recent price level (for instance a period of 10 of 10) by 10, period 9 of 10 by 9, period 8 of 10 by 8 , etc. Add the number you get for each period and then divide the outcome by the number of multiplies (10+9+8+7 etc).

Naturally this enables the EMA to react to recent price developments faster than the SMA, but it also increases the margin of error, because the earlier periods are mostly excluded from the calculation. The difference between the SMA and EMA increases when increasing the number of periods measured (say 20, 40, 65 etc).

Moving Averages Crossover Systems

When the price moves back and forth within a narrow channel (known as *oscillating*) the margin of error for Moving Averages increases considerably. Remember that, like all technical indicators, Moving Averages are by definition a little bit behind the times (like all technical indicators) and when prices quickly move back and forth, Moving Average predictions of future price movements become less accurate.

Many traders therefore use filters made up of several Moving Averages, looking for situations where these different MA's cross each other. These are called *Moving Averages crossover systems*.

Traders primarily look for moments when a short-term moving average crosses a longer-term moving average. When the short-term MA crosses the longer-term MA from *below*, a buy signal is generated, while a crossing from *above* generates a sell signal. Because these are signals for a price development that is already under way, it's often not the right move to actually buy and sell at the crossovers themselves.

The reason for this is that the actual crossover normally only takes place after a considerable up or down swing. Such a swing is often followed by what is called a *retracement* move, which recaptures part of the ground covered by the swing. Retracements like this are often caused by traders closing profitable positions to take profit, while others are trying to get in at the top or bottom of the move, driving the price in the opposite direction. Getting in at that moment often means buying the top and selling the bottom.

What's the point then?

The value of these kind of Moving Average filters lies in being able to determine what kind of trend the price action is currently involved in. When the short-term MA is above the longer-term MA, the price action is in an uptrend (i.e. the more recent the period measured, the higher the price) and vice versa. The crossover points to a possible trend reversal. The *'tight to wide 3 SMA trade'* explained below is an example of this.

3 SMA Filter

One well known filter is the 3 SMA filter, which is made up of 3 SMA's of different periods. Frequently measured periods for the 3 SMA are 3, 20 and 65. When the short term SMA is above the medium term SMA, which in turn is above the long term SMA, the price is clearly in an uptrend. Simply put: measured over the longest period the average price is X, over the medium term the price is X+1 and over the shortest period it's X+2. So, the more recent the period that is measured the higher the price.

While the 3 SMA filter shows the current trend, it doesn't tell you whether or not the trend will continue. Nevertheless it's an important tool for traders focussed on trending movements. The 3 SMA filter's main function is showing when you should *not* get in a trade. Are the SMA's very close together, or not in line with each other (short above medium, medium above long configuration)? Then the trend trader knows it's not the right time to get in, because there's no clear trend.

Tight to Wide 3 SMA Trade

There is an exception to the rule that the 3 SMA filter shouldn't be used for generating an entry signal (only for determining what kind of market we're currently in, uptrend, downtrend or range). This is when the 3 SMA's are close together and then start to run wider apart in the right alignment. That right alignment would be short above medium, medium above long in an uptrend, and vice versa in a downtrend.

The most important reason for this is that getting in at this point carries little risk but has a lot of potential. Why is there so little risk? Because there is little price difference when the short Moving Average crosses the medium Moving Average (the 3 SMA's were close together, remember). So there is less chance of retracement and even if retracement does occur, it will be minimal.

Now, the argument *not* to get in on the crossover was because it will only show you where the big swing occurs after it has already happened, with the added risk that retracement will come into play around the time the crossover takes place. But when the SMA's are close together and then start to fan out, there is little to fear from retracement.

The signal that is created makes for a good moment to get in. For an uptrend, the signal would be short-term prices that are higher than medium-term prices, which are higher than long-term prices. If the SMA lines move closer together again, right after they started running further apart, it could be concluded the fanning out of the SMA's was a false signal. However, you would have limited your risk by putting in relatively tight stops.

BOLLINGER BANDS

This is one of the most popular technical indicators.[20] One of the reasons for it is that Bollinger Bands (BB's) instantly show you when the price is deviating from its 'normal' trading channel. A lot of traders habitually run BB's on their candlestick charts.

For many traders, nothing beats riding the wave of a trend for as long as possible, like surfing in the green room. Opening a position on a nascent trend and then simply enjoying the ride of *The Long & Trending Road*, making you richer with every pip. As a range trader, you can get the same feeling with a good range trade, only the length of the one-directional price movement is of course much shorter in that case.

But when do we speak of a trend? And how do you spot it as quickly as possible? That's where Bollinger Bands come in. Bollinger Bands are based on the fact that prices move within a certain bandwidth about 70 – 80 percent of the time. When prices start to move **outside** this bandwidth, this could signify the beginning of a trend.

Bollinger Bands measure the *Standard Deviation* (SD) of the price, compared to the 20-period Moving Average. When BB's are close together it means market volatility is low, because the difference between the two extremes – Standard Deviation on the upside and the downside – is small.

In the next example, BB's are relatively far apart, meaning price volatility is high, making it harder to predict the market direction.

---

20   Bollinger Bands were developed by John A. Bollinger, a financial analyst in the early 1980s. The standard work about this technical indicator is Bollinger on Bollinger Bands, from 2002, by John Bollinger.

Bollinger Bands GBP/USD sept/okt 2006

Using Bollinger Bands to Open and Close Positions

To use Bollinger Bands successfully when trading on the forex, three questions are important:

1. Trend detection -- when can we say a trend is emerging?
2. Entry point -- when to open a position?
3. Exit point -- when is the trend considered to have run its course?

Of these three questions, the third is – surprisingly perhaps – the most important. The value of exit points is often underestimated by traders. Most traders are primarily concerned with entry points. Which stock, commodity or currency should I buy? When should I go long the euro? Of course it's important to pick a good moment to get in on a trade, but the reason most beginning traders are losing money is because they a) don't known how to limit their losses and b) don't know how to capitalize on their winning trades. Both a and b are determined by finding suitable exit points (note: we'll take a closer look at exit points later on in the book).

Trend Detection -- When Can We Say a Trend Is Emerging?

When using Bollinger Bands, a possible trend is said to be emerging when the candlestick closes above the upper BB or below the lower BB. Keep in mind however, that merely touching or crossing the band is not enough. A closing above / below the Band increases the chance of a possible definitive breach (as far as anything is ever definitive in financial trading).

Entry Point -- When to Open a Position?

Even if the candle closes in the buy / sell zone (outside the BB channel) we still don't open a position right away. Why not? Because we're always looking for low-risk propositions. The difference between profitable and unprofitable traders is much less a case of being able to 'pick a winner' and much more one of cutting your losses and letting your profits run. That's why it's generally better to wait for prices to retrace, before getting in.

There is almost always some retracement following a rally. Even in a huge bull market, traders take profit while others get in on the opposite side because they think the price is bottoming/peaking. Successful traders often get in after a retracement. They don't try to cause trends (try the fashion industry if that's your thing) they try to follow them.

Getting in only after retracement has taken place can limit your risk exposure on a position considerably. If the price continues to move away from the high/low – meaning the retracement doesn't stop, thus turning into a reversal – there wasn't really a trend to begin with, saving you a stopped out position, (because you would only get in after retracement has taken place). Traders who opened a position immediately when the first candle closed in the buy / sell zone, no longer have that luxury. An added bonus is that if indeed there was retracement and the price returns to the buy/sell zone, your profit is greater if you get in after retracement has taken place. The only negative to this tactic is that every once in a while you'll miss a trade, because there is no retracement at all. Though this is obviously disappointing, it happens only rarely. Additionally, you should keep in mind that the goal of a successful trader is not getting in on every single profitable trade. The goal is – or should be – keeping Expected Value (EV) as high as possible and risk exposure as low as possible.

Therefore, we only open a position after the price momentarily returns inside the channel. If the candle closed substantially outside the buy / sell zone, the price only has to touch the BB when retracing, but either way we only get in when the price has temporarily retraced. This way, you'll limit losses in case the trend doesn't follow through, something which happens more often than not. You will also increase profits when a trend *does* form (because you got in at a better price).

On rare occasions, there will be hardly any retracement and the trend forms right away, causing you to miss a profitable trade. Not a very pleasant situation of course, but console yourself with the knowledge that in the long term, you will make more money by waiting for the retracement.

Exit Point -- When is the Trend Considered to Have Run Its Course?

As said, this is the most important question, because it can both limit your losses and increase your profits. Many novice traders learn soon enough of the old adage, '*Cut your losses and let your profits run*'. It's considered one of the golden rules of trading (another famous one: "*Greed is good.*" – Gordon Gekko in *Wall Street*). So, why are there so many losing traders if everybody knows this rule? The obvious answer -- because it's so hard to follow.

What is the greatest temptation after losing a lot of money in the casino or at the poker table? Increasing the stakes, to win back your losses. For most people, it's in their nature to do exactly the opposite of cutting losses and letting their profits run. Instead, they let their losses run and cut their profits short. Of course having difficulty accepting losses is very natural, as is the urge to want to lock in realized profits. After all, seeing realized profits being vaporized is a terrible thing, and seeing them turn into a loss is even worse.

The good news is that carefully considering and putting in place exit points can prevent this. As long as you stick to them of course....

The exit point when working with Bollinger Bands is usually when the price touches the opposite band. So in case of an uptrend, the touching of the lower Bollinger Band would create an exit signal. Why not the crossing of the Band or the closing of a candle below the Band? That's a matter of limiting risk exposure. A trend that's not strong enough to stay above the opposite Band can't really be called a trend and isn't worth taking any risk for anymore. (to use another saying, this one borrowed from the noble game of poker -- *you should know when to release a shitty hand*).

The correct use of Bollinger Bands not only increases the chance of spotting a trend and exploiting it successfully, but also forces one to think about exit points (both for taking profit and cutting losses). This helps foster a more planned approach to trading, which in turn increases the chances of developing a profitable trading strategy.

RELATIVE STRENGTH INDEX

This is a fairly simple, but much used technical indicator. The *Relative Strength Index*[21] (RSI) measures the relative strength of a trend. The RSI helps to better estimate what to expect of a (possible) trend, increasing the chance of successfully getting in on one.

---

21   Developed by J. Welles Wilder, who first wrote about it in 1978, in the book New Concepts in Technical Trading Systems.

How the RSI Works

The RSI measures the strength of a price development by comparing the number of times a currency pair closes higher to the number of times it closes lower. This is usually done over 14 periods, whereby the data is weighed through the use of exponential averages; in other words, the more recent the data, the more it counts.

The result is a number between 0 and 100. A rating above 70 indicates an overbought situation, while a rating below 30 indicates an oversold situation.

A rating above 70 or below 30 does not mean you have to spring into action right away; it only shows that the price has now entered an overbought/oversold situation, and that a change in this could signify a trend reversal.

How to Use the Relative Strength Index

A much used method when using the RSI is to compare it with the actual price action. For instance, when prices keep making higher highs while the RSI does not, it signifies a trend reversal or possible consolidation. The same goes for down trends, when prices keep making lower lows but the RSI does not.

Divergence

Spotting the difference between price action and momentum is known as *divergence*. It is a method that works well with several technical indicators. At first sight, everything looks hunky dory with the trend, because prices keep trending higher (or lower, in case of a down trend), but the technical indicator shows that the trend is fact already weakening.

To quickly spot this kind of divergence, traders often use simple trend line analysis, connecting highs/lows directly on the RSI. When that RSI trend line is falling while the price itself is still rising, it's a strong indication that what is called *trend line exhaustion* is close-by. The next chart illustrates an example of trend line exhaustion.

RSI Divergence EUR/USD Sept 2008

The main advantage of the RSI is that it filters out market noise. Price developments can be hugely volatile, especially in the short term, making them very unpredictable. Because the RSI takes multiple periods into account and weighs recent periods more heavily than earlier ones, the chance of false signals is much smaller. The RSI can therefore help you find the right moment to open the position and increase your chance of a successful trade.

STOCHASTICS

This is a somewhat older, but still popular technical indicator.[22] The core idea of stochastics is that in an uptrend, the closing prices for each period are always close to the high – because the bulls keep raising the price – while the opposite is true for a downtrend, when the bears keep selling. It's an idea both simple and logical. What the stochastics formula does, is show how far along the trend probably is.

Range Trading Tool

As said, the price development of currency pairs is *range-bound* 70 to 80 percent of the time, meaning the price stays within a channel made up of resistance on the upside and support on the downside, going back and forth without much happening. For the real trend trader these are not the most exciting moments, but for those who know how to capitalize on it, range trading can be a goldmine. The main advantage of ranging prices is of course that the directional predictability is fairly high. This enables the range trader to work

22   Developed by Dr. George Lane in the 1950s.

with tight stops, while the chance of success is high.

For example, let's say that the price moves in a range of 25 pips and you're getting in on the bottom side of the range and out on the top side. Do this 80 percent of the time and you could profit nicely. Suppose you execute 10 trades, using stops of 25 pips. You would earn 200 pips (8 x 25 pips) and lose only 50 pips (2 x 25). Deduct 10 x 2 pips for the spread (10 trades) and you would pocket a net profit of 130 pips, or 13 pips per trade on average. Not bad at all.

Determining approximately where you are in the range of the price action, is where Stochastics comes in. Keep in mind though that you should never trust Stochastics blindly (something that goes for all technical indicators) but merely use it as a hint, as another argument for putting on a trade, or for deciding against it.

Stochastics Explained

Stochastics gets its core data from measuring the Moving Average level, usually over 14 periods. There are fast stochastics and slow stochastics.

Fast stochastics measures the price compared to the 14 period Moving Average, and rates it on a scale of 1 to 100. Slow stochastics is the 3 period average of the fast stochastics. The advantage of slow stochastics is that it filters out market noise even more than fast stochastics does. Unfortunately, it also shows more *lag* because of this.

Stochastics moves between a value of 1 and 100. The stochastics number for a given price therefore shows you at where the price is, compared to the 14 period Moving Average. So if the stochastics for a given price reads 50, it means the price is exactly in the middle of the 14 period Moving Average.

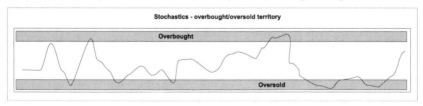

The basic rule states that when stochastics reads at 80 or above, prices are in an overbought phase (making a price decline more likely). Inversely, a reading of 20 or less indicates an oversold phase (making a price rise more likely).

That doesn't mean you should go short immediately after the stochastics reads over 80, or long when it's under 20. A high reading of 80 or above, or a low reading of less than 20, can easily persist for a longer period of time. The idea is to keep an eye on the indicator and wait for it to break the 80 or 20 line **again**, signaling a reversal.

In essence, stochastics is a momentum-meter. Used correctly – as described above – it will show you when a trend reversal has started.

Stochastics at its Best: Divergence

One of the best ways to use stochastics is by looking for a divergence situation – during an overbought/oversold (80/20) phase – when prices keep making higher highs/lower lows, while the Stochastics is already moving back to the 80/20 line but has not crossed it yet. In that case we would have a divergence between the price action and stochastics, which signals a possible trend exhaustion. With this method you would not be hindered by the indicator lagging behind real time action because the already falling/rising indicator predicts that the current trend might soon be over.

Again, no TI can ever give you 100 percent certainty about the future direction of a price development (nor can any fundamental analysis for that matter). The trick is to find low-risk possibilities, where you have a relatively small chance of a losing trade and a relatively high chance of a winning one. Succeeding at this can make you a lot of money in the long term.

FIBONACCI

One of the most popular technical indicators, Fibonacci ratios are used by many traders. This makes it essential for you to know how they work. After all, markets are driven by people.

The Fibonacci sequence is the most esoteric technical indicator we look at in this book. It is esoteric in that it really has nothing to do with market movements as such and that there is no rational explanation for why the Fibonacci sequence should be applicable to the financial market. Devout supporters of the Fibonacci ratios – of which there are many – will nevertheless fervently deny the irrationality of its use. Due to their numbers, it is important that you know what all the hubbub is about.

That the Fibonacci sequence is often visible in price developments is doubtlessly true. Important resistance and support levels can often be predicted with the help of Fibonacci levels. The reasons for this are not born out of any mystical power however, but are much more mundane.

Everyone who is trying to predict the future (and as traders, we all are) risks losing himself in all kinds of *holy grail* stories about that one particle / being / astrological event / indicator that can explain all about people, the world and everything in it.

Perhaps you think I'm exaggerating about the methods traders use to try and predict future price developments, but some go much further than a little drooling over the Fibonacci sequence. They look for influences on human behavior in such things as tidal movements and sun spots that influence Earth's magnetic radiation (which in turn supposedly influences human behavior) and so on and so forth. It seems many people simply want to believe there is a higher order to everything that drives us.

The reason for this long introduction about the Fibonacci sequence – which is definitely important for a trader to know about – is because it is also the last technical indicator we'll discuss in this book, making for a good moment to emphasize once again not to overestimate the usability of TI's.

At the end of the day, markets are driven by human behavior. Everything that influences human behavior is important, including technical indicators – even irrational technical indicators – but at the same time no market is immune to substantial changes in the intrinsic values that underly market prices. When the American economy performs substantially worse than the economy of the Eurozone for a significant period of time, the value of the euro will rise compared to the US dollar. There are, after all, economic values at the core of the EUR/USD rate. Technical indicators can help you determine the strength of a price development, or predict the probable end of a trend, but in the long term the direction of a currency pair is determined by the economic values that underlie each currency.

It's also important to realize that many traders use technical indicators and fundamentals just to find good entry points, while successful trading only depends about 10% on being able to find good entry points. Exit points, position sizing (i.e. determining the maximum risk exposure for a trade) and expected value are much more important for trading profitably on the forex. All of which we will discuss this further on in the book.

So, Finally, What Is the Fibonacci Sequence

Leonardo of Pisa (1170 – 1250) better known as Fibonacci, discovered that a number sequence constructed with a certain formula – $Fn = F(n+1) + F(n-2)$ – possesses interesting mathematical characteristics. The beginning of the sequence is as follows:

0,1,2,3,4,5,6,13,21,34,55,89,144,233,377,610,987,1597

The most interesting characteristic is that the ratio of neighboring numbers in the sequence is always 0,618. (though this is not the case for the smaller numbers by the way). This ratio is called phi, a.k.a the Golden Ratio. Another interesting fact is that the reversed ratio of the same neighboring numbers is

1,618; or 1 + phi.

Example:

144/233 = 0,618

233/144 = 1,618

To stress its importance, supporters of the Fibonacci sequence frequently point to the fact that the Golden Ratio is found everywhere in nature. Some traders seem to believe that something that plays such an important role as a natural ratio must also be a significant factor in the financial markets. (perhaps because the markets are driven by people – who in turn are part of nature?).

Extra: in 2001, Donald Simanek, a physics professor at the University of Pennsylvania, published 'Science Askew', which invalidated a lot of the Fibonacci Ratio examples that were said to be found in nature. Among other things, he describes his examination of the supposed 'phi' ratio between someone's entire length and the length from a person's navel to their feet; a well-known phi ratio. What made Simanek's examination all the more interesting – at least for 50 percent of us – was that he used female swimsuit models for it. Simanek went on to prove two things with his 'phi ratio in swimsuit models' research:

The swimsuit models did not possess the well-known phi ratio.

Even physics professors can meet swimsuit models; they just need to find a good excuse for it.

How the Fibonacci Sequence Works in Trading

In the FX market, traders concentrate on the following Fibonacci levels:

0,382 (1 – phi ratio 0,618)

0,5 (which, by the way, is **not** a real Fibonacci ratio!)

0,618 (phi)

1,382 (Fibonacci extension ratio)

1,618 (Fibonacci extension ratio)

Fibonacci Support Levels in an Uptrend

The classic method to apply Fibonacci (Fib) ratios in technical analysis is by drawing a trend line from the lowest point to the highest point in an uptrend (opposite in a downtrend) and then place Fib lines on 38,2%, 50% and 61,8% of the total move. These Fib lines are said to represent strong support levels in case of a retracement from the highest point downward.

Fibonacci Extension Ratios

When there is a price breakout – for instance beyond an ascending triangle (see chapter 12) – Fibonacci extension ratios are used to determine how far the breakout will likely stretch. The trader calculates the vertical distance of the ascending triangle and then multiplies that with the Fibonacci extension ratios to determine possible exit points.

The most commonly used extension ratios are 138,2%, 161,8%, 261,8% and 423,6%. Most traders use Fibonacci extension levels in combination with other technical indicators and/or chart patterns, to get more input about good exit points.

Apart from Fibonacci, it's never a bad idea to split your position in two or three parts. You don't have to put on those two or three positions at the same time, but could instead opt to 'grow into' the entire position. The idea here is to open a second and possibly a third position when the price continues to move in your direction. This would prevent you from risking too much before the trend has proven itself a bit more.

Another advantage of growing into a position is that it also enables you to grow out of a position. You could, for instance, put in different exit points, with profit targets that are increasingly ambitious. Advice from professional traders frequently includes this idea of several exit points, which are sometimes based on Fibonacci extension ratios.

Why Fibonacci Is Important in FX Trading

In part, the answer to this question is pretty obvious. Like every market, the forex is driven by human behavior. Even the automatic trading models you can build or buy are based on human suppositions. The human factor is everywhere and many, many traders are well aware of the Fibonacci levels. And whether or not they believe in them, they know that other traders are aware of them too, which increases their importance.

Many traders grow into their positions gradually, as described above, which can somewhat resemble the fib levels at 30% and 60% of the trend. When gradually growing into a trade, traders first wait until the move has started and then put on a relatively small position (half, or 1/3 of the desired position for instance) and then grow into a complete position if the move continues. Combined with multiple profit targets and stops, traders run less risk this way, while maximizing their chances of a decent profit.

PART IV

FOREX TRADING STRATEGIES

CHAPTER 15 TREND TRADING

The concept of trend trading is easy to understand and very popular among forex traders. A good trend can be spotted by anyone on a chart (in the absence of a clear trend, prices are by definition *ranging*). Many forex strategies are based on trend trading, but successful application of it requires solid discipline.

WHAT IS A TREND

In the financial world, a trend is a clearly visible direction in the price development of a financial product. (be it currency pairs, or futures, stocks, bonds, options or other financial instruments). For instance, take a look at the next chart, which represents the price development of oil. The chart clearly shows trending in the oil price. First, oil is pushed to a price above $140 a barrel in a clear trend. But then, an abrupt trend reversal takes place and the price falls sharply, to a level below $50 a barrel.[23]

Oil Price 2007 - 2008 in USD

During an uptrend, prices continue to make higher highs, while in a downtrend they continue to make lower lows. Obviously there are temporary setbacks, called *retracement*, but the general direction is clear. A successful trader once said he used to print out a chart, put it on the wall of his study and then sit back and study it from a couple of meters away. If he could spot a clear trend on the chart he would get in on the trade, if not, then no go. Rudimentary, yes, but nevertheless effective (though on the downside, he has since had to start

---

23 The trend reversal in the oil price had already started when, on September 15, 2008, Lehman Brothers crumbled and the worldwide financial crisis 'officially' started. As a result, the worldwide demand for oil plummeted, as did the oil price.

wearing glasses)

According to most technical analysts, currency pairs move within a relatively small bandwidth 70 to 80 percent of the time. That is one of the reasons why so many traders use Bollinger Bands for their technical analysis, because it's a very useful indicator for predicting patterns within a certain bandwidth. So in reality, prices are moving sideways – *ranging* – much more often than they are trending. That makes successful trend trading difficult, but also potentially very profitable.

TREND TRADING STRATEGY

The goal for a trend trader is simple: try to get in when the trend has just started and then stay with it until the price action turns again in a trend reversal. The basic assumption for the trend trader is that the price keeps moving in the direction it was moving when he put the trade on. If true, a trend would indeed exist and the trade would be a success. If not, a trend apparently does not yet exist, and the trader should not be in the trade.

This sounds simple of course (and it basically is) but it also means that by definition, a trend trader gets into many positions that die out quickly, stopping him out for small losses.

Yes, you can put your stops further away and get stopped out less often, but this risks eating away at your Expected Value per trade. Often, the success of a good trend trading strategy is about accepting many small losses in exchange for one big winner. The successful trend trader knows this and has the discipline to endure it.

A trend trader who risks 30 pips per position to win 1500 and finally gets in on a successful trade after 15 failed attempts, loses 15 x 30 pips and wins 1500 pips with that one, fantastic trade. So he'll lose 450 pips but wins 1500. If we deduct an average of 3 pips spread per trade, the trader would still have a net profit of 1002 pips over 16 trades, or 63 pips per trade. Not bad at all!

Sounds good, no? Still, this kind of trend trading is not for everybody. It can be quite frustrating to have to put on 15 losing trades without knowing for sure that that 16th trade is indeed the fat, profitable one. The temptation to believe the 'this trend will start any moment' whispers of your emotional self grows, trying to persuade you to place those stops further and further away. Even worse, you might be tempted to leave them out altogether (after all, you're right and 'they' are wrong). Give in to this, and the fairy tale will not end with the boy/girl that made a million dollars trading, but with a depleted forex account.

Therefore, every forex trader looking to specialize himself as a trend trader, would do well to start by looking himself squarely in the eye (preferably in front of a mirror) and ask if he could take 10 losses for every winner. And don't forget you will also have to resist the temptation of cashing out too quickly on that winning trade, accepting 300 pips in profit when it could have been 1500.

But not to worry if trend trading is not your thing; there are plenty of other trading strategies for you to become highly successful in.

CHAPTER 16 RANGE TRADING

Range trading is only interesting when markets are relatively calm. Picture for yourself a currency pair with a price development that resembles a little creek, happily meandering back and forth between clear resistance and support levels, without settling itself on a clear direction. As a trader, you could identify those resistance and support levels and pick trade triggers, stop losses and profit targets based on those levels. That is range trading in a nutshell.

THE NUTS AND BOLTS OF RANGE TRADING

Range trading is putting on positions with the intent to profit from temporary ranging movements of a financial product. Although nothing beats the thrill of being on the right side of a trade when prices explode in break out trading – and the profit per trade in range trading is often less spectacular – your chances of success are much higher with range trading. Check out the next chart to get a quick idea of what range trading is all about.

This is a candlestick chart of the EUR/CHF, an old favorite of range traders, because its price action is so often sideways. (A notable exception was 2011, when the franc attracted many investors seeking a safe haven after trouble began surrounding the eurozone. This pushed the franc ever higher against the euro, until the Swiss National Bank decided to intervene on the forex)

That example notwithstanding, the usual ranging of the Swiss franc has everything to do with the fact that the Swiss economy is very dependent on the Eurozone (almost all Swiss exports go to the Eurozone). A not surprising fact, given that Switzerland is surrounded by EU countries. This dependence normally ensures a very stable relationship between the two economies and their currencies.

Range Trading EUR/CHF 2004-2005

The daily chart of the EUR/CHF usually shows a clear channel. When you've identified this channel, putting on a trade after the bounce back from a resistance/support level has a fairly high chance of success.

Range trading can work equally well in futures trading. Take a look at the next chart, showing the rate of the S&P 500 between January and July 2011 on a daily basis.

Split Range S&P 500 jan-juli 2011

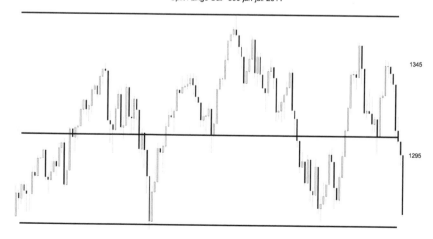

Even though the range lying between the horizontal lines is broken a couple of times, traders can be relatively certain that when the price is within the range, the movement – up or down – will be completed.

How to Recognize a Possible Range Trade

You can only spot a currency pair's ranging movement after it's already been going on for a while, because resistance and support levels have to be formed first. There are, however, a couple of tips that can help you quicker recognize the ranging movement in a currency pair more quickly.

1. After a period of volatility there is a greater chance that a ranging movement will be reestablished. Currency pairs often start ranging after a period of volatility due to the split among traders on which direction the pair is going to go. All possibilities are open. Will the price continue in the direction of the breakout or, on the contrary, fall back to the original price level before the breakout. On a candlestick chart this is often visible through what is known as a *flag chart* pattern. See the next chart for an example of a flag pattern of the USD/CAD.

USD/CAD april 2011

2. Ranging is more common in currency pairs with little difference in interest rates, set by the central banks of the respective currencies. This is the opposite of the carry trade (see chapter 20) where the trader is looking for currency pairs with big differences in interest rates between the underlying currencies.

3. The greater the interdependency between the economies that are underlying the currencies of a given currency pair, the bigger the chance that such a currency pair will often have ranging price action. Think for instance about the EUR/CHF and the Swiss export that mostly goes to the Eurozone.

4. Study earlier periods of a specific currency pair on a chart. Was there much ranging going on? And if so, what was the bandwidth of the ranging movement? And how long did it remain in place? This kind of information can help you make a quick estimation whether or not a new range is forming for the currency pair.

HOW DO YOU SET UP A RANGE TRADING STRATEGY

To set up a successful range trading strategy you have to go through a couple of steps.

Identify the Range

There are several methods you can use to identify a ranging movement, but the easiest one is to simply use Bollinger Bands and your own common sense. Get the chart of the time frame you plan to trade on and look for the resistance and support levels. If the price has bounced back from a resistance and support level at least once, a ranging movement might be forming.

Identify the Entry Point for the Trade (a.k.a. the Trigger)

A good entry point for a range trade is the first candle that brings the price **back within the channel again**, after it had broken through first. Should the price break through that same resistance/support again, after you put on the position, the stop loss would eject you from the trade. Your job when formulating a working set-up for a range trade is to find an entry point where all the lights are green for go, where your risk exposure is minimal and your chances of success optimal.

Set a Stop Loss and Profit Target

Put your stop loss somewhat past the high point/low point that the price reached earlier, when it broke through the resistance/support. Remember, your hypothesis is that the price will start ranging again; should it break through that resistance/support level again, to reach an even higher high/lower low, your hypothesis would have been proven wrong and you should exit the trade.

Put your profit target just past the resistance/support level on the other side of the range, where – if all goes well – the price is heading. Your hypothesis here is that the price will first move somewhat beyond the resistance/support level, before moving back within the range again.

Don't Chase the Breakout When Your Stop Loss Is Triggered

It can be very tempting to open a position that trades the supposed breakout which triggered your stop loss. The idea in this case would be that the triggering of your stop loss by definition constitutes a breakout. This is nonsense of course, but to some traders being stopped out by what looks to be an explosive breakout is more than they can bear. And of course it seems that the quickest way to regain the money you lost on the position would be to catch the wave of that (possible) breakout. It would also be the stupidest way.

For while it's always possible that you have been stopped out by a genuine breakout, in most cases you'll simply compound losses by half-heartedly trading a breakout that could easily turn out to be a *false* breakout (in fact, it will be most of the time). Therefore, once you have set-up a range trade, it's better to take a step back when you have been stopped out and have another look at what the most likely price development will be.

CHAPTER 17 SCALPING

Scalping[24] is a strategy in which positions are kept open only for a very short period of time, in order to pick up a lot of small profits. This can be a highly profitable way of trading the forex.

How long the position is kept open varies from a couple of seconds to 2 minutes at most. If kept open longer it's no longer called scalping, but intra-day trading. The targeted profit per trade usually lies between 1 and 5 pips net (i.e. what is left after paying the spread). It's possible to set up a scalping strategy that targets profits between 5 and 15 pips net, but the position then often needs to be kept open for longer than 2 minutes.

NOT A GOOD STRATEGY FOR BEGINNERS

Scalping is often done with high leverage, because it only pays to go after profits of just a couple of pips when those pips are worth something. Working with Micro Lots for instance (where 1 pip is worth about 10 cents) it wouldn't be very lucrative to develop a strategy where the average net profit per trade is 1 pip. However, with Standard Lots, where pips are $10 each, you could make a nice living at 1 pip a minute.

One of the biggest mistakes beginning traders make is trying to maximize their profits by using leverage in a way that ignores all solid risk management. (imagine depositing $200 and then trading Mini Lots, 1 pip = $1, using 500:1 leverage). This is an almost certain path to going bust as a trader. Since scalping only gets interesting when trading bigger lot sizes, beginning traders – with beginner size trading capitals – could quickly use up their bankroll.

Another reason this strategy is not really suitable for beginning traders is that it requires a lot of discipline and stress management to execute correctly. A single emotional trade can wipe out the carefully accumulated profits of an entire day, and a trader going on tilt could even lose days worth of profits.

Yes, you can set stop losses to protect yourself somewhat against losing too much on a single trade, but most scalpers don't like stops, because it takes too long to set them. Profit targets aren't commonly used either. Apart from the time it takes to set them they also keep the scalper from profiting on the occasional *spike* – which can push the price to double digit pip profits in a short ride. Experienced scalpers are therefore using either an automated system or a quick, vigilant eye and a steady hand on the mouse.

---

24   The term scalping is also used for a certain fraudulent form of market manipulation, as well as for a legitimate form of arbitrage. However, as far as the scope of this book goes, scalping refers to the trading strategy that aims to profit from small price changes in very short periods of time.

HOW SCALPING WORKS

First, you will need a working strategy. The most important part of every scalping strategy is risk management. A profitable scalping strategy risks only a small part of the total trading capital and quickly secures small profits.

Successful scalping means risking 1 or 2 percent of your trading capital at most, never more. Working with small profit margins simply does not allow room for big losses.

The profitable scalper develops a solid trading strategy that he will not deviate from. This is one of the reasons why scalping on the forex is increasingly done with the help of automated systems (a.k.a forex bots, or expert advisors – EA's). Automated trading effectively eliminates human emotions and its inevitable missteps.

Does this mean that forex bots will make you rich as a forex scalper? Not necessarily of course, because you will still have to teach this automated system what parameters it should follow, and to be able to do that you will need to know what you're doing.

IS SCALPING THE HOLY GRAIL?

No. There is no holy grail of trading, plain and simple. The sooner you realize this, the sooner you can start developing your own profitable trading strategy. But before you begin working on a strategy based on scalping, you should familiarize yourself thoroughly with peripherals like money management, risk management and trading discipline.

Although scalping is often a slayer of beginners, it can be very profitable for experienced traders who are willing to devote the time and effort needed to set up a solid system.

CHAPTER 18 BREAKOUT TRADING

Breakout trading strategies are based on entering the market when prices have broken through resistance/support levels. There are many different breakout strategies and they're used in all financial markets.

Breakout strategies are especially popular among beginning forex traders, because they are easy to understand and execute. The basic idea is to enter the market as soon as the price breaks through the channel and starts trading outside it. A commonly used technical indicator for spotting breakouts is the Bollinger Bands indicator. When the price breaks above the upper or lower Bollinger Band, it is seen as an increased chance of a breakout.

In its simplest form, a breakout strategy involves placing a buy stop or sell stop either above the resistance or below the support level. A buy stop is an order for a long position that is only filled when a certain price is reached. A sell stop order works the same way, but in this case a short position is opened when a given price is reached.

EXAMPLE OF A BREAKOUT STRATEGY

Suppose the currency pair EUR/USD has moved in a range between 1,4300 and 1,4500 for the past few days. The 1,4500 has proved to be an important resistance level, and the 1,4300 and important support level. The trader now places a buy stop order at $1,4510 and a sell stop at $1,4290. This means that if the price breaks the 1,4500 and touches the 1,4510, a long position would be opened that can profit optimally from a bullish breakout. In the same manner a short position would be opened if the price breaks 1,4300 and touches 1,4290.

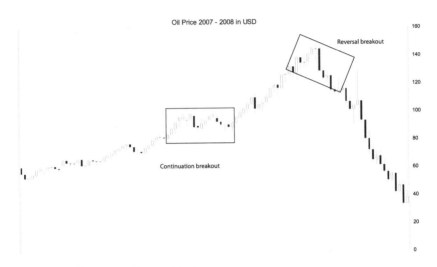

Oil Price 2007 - 2008 in USD

DIFFERENT KINDS OF BREAKOUTS

There are basically two kinds of breakouts, the *continuation breakout* and the *reversal breakout*.

Continuation breakout: a breakout is called a continuation breakout when the price continues to move in the direction it was moving before a period of consolidation. Think of a temporary price range, when buyers and sellers wind down their positions and try to predict which way the price will go. The oil price chart above shows an example of a continuation breakout.

Reversal breakout: A reversal breakout is the beginning of a real trend reversal. In other words, the price development breaks with the previous trend and starts trending in the reverse direction. This is usually caused by changed fundamentals. See the oil price chart for a reversal breakout example as well.

Naturally the reversal breakout is rarer than the continuation breakout, simply because trend reversals themselves are much less common than the continuation of an existing trend after a (usually short) period of consolidation.

There are all kinds of breakout strategies, both for the intra-day trader and the long-term forex trader who puts on positions for weeks, months or even years.

The most important characteristic of the breakout strategy is that the currency pair has to have left the channel it had been moving in. To determine the range of the channel you have to look at its resistance and support levels. There are several ways to gain insight into the resistance and support levels, the simplest of which is open to everyone.

For instance, take a candlestick chart of the 10 minute EUR/USD (where every candle represents 10 minutes). Now review the high and low for a period of about 20 – 30 candles, and determine whether they have been reached (but not broken) more than once. If the answer is yes, you could say that short term resistance- and support levels are formed by that respective high and low. If this high or low is broken, it would be a breakout.

The core element of each breakout strategy is entering the market when the price breaks through a certain resistance or support level, i.e. out of its 'normal' channel (remember the Bollinger Bands). Breakthroughs like that can be the beginning of very lucrative trades.

So why aren't breakout strategies the holy grail of trading systems either? The answer is obvious: because not all breakouts push on. In fact, most breakouts don't push on. So called *'false breakouts'* break through resistance and support levels, but cannot hold on to their momentum; they can't force a sustained break. (some traders say that a break is a break when the price moves through a resistance/support barrier, but most traders make a distinction between *technical breaks* and *sustained breaks*).

For instance, when the EUR/USD has been unable to break the 1,4448 in two successive attempts but the third time a short spike pushes it to 1,4451, does that mean resistance has been broken? Technically yes, but most of the time the resistance will still spring into action and push the price back, because many traders put on positions against the breakout as soon as resistance/support has been broken. Trading strategies based on this are called *breakout fading* strategies, because they speculate against the direction of the breakout.

TESTING A BREAKOUT

Obviously you don't want to open a position meant to profit from a breakout when there is a big chance of it being a false breakout. To minimize this chance you could first test if the breakout is real. The two most commonly used methods for this are secondary resistance/support levels and role reversals, which we will look at now.

1. **Secondary resistance/support levels**. In essence, this is nothing more than deciding on a second line of defense the price has to break, before the break of the first level is considered a success. To do this you study the charts you use for your trading strategy. When you're an intra-day trader for instance, rarely keeping trades open longer than an hour or two, you would probably look at the 5 minute candlestick chart. For an intra-day trade on the EUR/USD, a second line of defense of about 15 pips beyond the specific resistance/support is a sign that a breakout might last longer.

2. **Role Reversal**. This is the transformation from a broken resistance into a support (as well as a broken support into a resistance). The idea is as simple as it is elegant. When the price breaks through a certain resistance, that resistance automatically becomes a new support. If the price retraces but doesn't break the new support, it's a sign that the breakout is real, because the price has not returned to the channel it was in before the breakout. It's very commonly the case that the price pivots around newly established support/resistance levels, but every time there is a bounce off (i.e. the price touching, or almost touching the limit, but not breaking through) it's a stronger sign that the new support/resistance is in place and the breakout is real.

CHAPTER 19 FADING THE BREAKOUT

Some traders put on their best positions when the breakout of a currency pair *cannot* sustain itself. Trading strategies based on these false breakouts (a.k.a *fakeouts*) bet against the breakout.

EXAMPLE OF BREAKOUT FADING

The simplest example of a breakout fading strategy is opening a position the moment the price retraces below the former resistance or above the former support (following an earlier breakthrough).

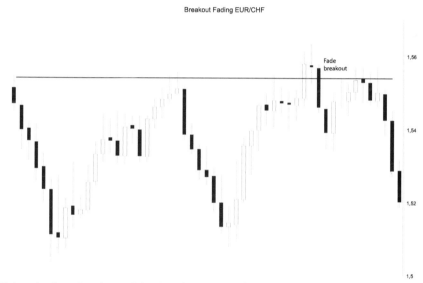

Breakout Fading EUR/CHF

Take a look at the chart of the EUR/CHF. First, the price boldly breaks through its resistance. It had done so before, but not so forcefully.

Now the trader that wants to fade the breakout waits. If the breakout pushes on it will be bad luck for him, or in any case his set-up will not be triggered and he won't open a position. However, should the price fall back below the former resistance line (which is now, in effect, the new support) he will open a trade.

As it happens, the price does indeed retrace in the example above, and the position is opened. After a short push upward, the price falls back again, this time far below the resistance line, pocketing the breakout fader a nice profit.

SHORT TERM TRADING STRATEGY

Fading the breakout is usually most effective as a short term trading strategy. It can work as a long term strategy as well, but when prices break through a resistance on a weekly chart it's much more significant than when they break one on a 15 min chart.

Most breakouts fail. This is understandable, because they are trying to break resistance and support levels that were identified as resistance and support for a reason. The bulls or bears (depending on it being about a resistance or a support, respectively) had trouble breaking through those levels at least once before, or perhaps they represent important psychological barriers, like the 1,4000 and 1,5000 barrier for the EUR/USD.

The most interesting thing about breakout fading strategies is that they basically jump on the wagon of a recently confirmed hypothesis, namely that a certain resistance/support level turns out to be too strong again. Where the real breakout can only get real confirmation after having pushed on for some time, a false breakout can be determined with greater certainty when the resistance/support in question turns out to have been too strong.

Real breakouts can be very lucrative. This fact and the simple logic behind them makes breakout trading very popular with beginning traders. But more experienced traders often prefer a breakout fading strategy, because it offers clearer entry signals and has a statistically higher chance of success.

CHAPTER 20 THE CARRY TRADE

The carry trade is a strategy that involves the selling of a financial product that carries a low interest, and the buying of a financial product that carries a higher interest. Although you would have to pay interest on the product you sold, you receive interest on the product that carries the higher interest.

In times of economic stability, the carry trade is very popular on the forex. This has everything to do with high leverage and the daily interest payments (known as rollover rates) that are common[25] in the currency trade.

The reason economic stability is important for a carry trade, is that you don't want the currencies you have positions in to be involved in too much action. Carry trade positions on the currency market are held first and foremost to profit from interest rate differences, not from price developments in the currency pairs themselves (though of course those profits would be very welcome too). Because if the price moves against you, the whole advantage of the carry trade could be wiped out. So you are definitely looking to avoid any surprises that could upset – and possibly reverse – the bigger trend.

HOW THE CARRY TRADE WORKS

In currency trading, the carry trade is the selling of a currency that carries a low interest and the buying of a currency that carries a high interest. You *pay* interest on the currency that carries a low interest and *receive* interest on the currency that carries a high interest. The difference between the high and low interest is called the *positive carry*.

Most – but not all – brokers charge and pay interest on positions that remain open at the end of the day. The broker closes and reopens the position and credits or debits the difference in overnight interest rates between the two currencies involved in the position. These are the costs for 'carrying' the position to the next day. This is also known as rolling over, with the overnight interest rate being the rollover rate.

Note: With a short position of 10.000 units on the GBP/USD, you would **pay** interest for 'borrowing' – remember it's a short position – $10,000 in British Pounds. You'd **receive** interest on buying $10,000 in US Dollars. If the British interest rate is higher than the US rate, there would be a negative carry. Should the British interest rate be the lower one, you would have a positive carry. So, when you keep a position open that sells a currency with a high interest and

---

25   Not every forex broker pays or charges rollover rates for currency positions that are kept open longer than 24 hours. Ask your broker about this if you are interested in the carry trade and/or want to keep positions open longer than 24 hours.

buys a currency with a low interest, you'd have to pay interest. If it's the other way around, you would receive interest.

The kicker is, that because working with high leverage is common on the forex, you could pocket high interest yields on capital you don't actually have to put on the table to open the position. With 400:1 leverage for example, you could open a GBP/USD position of 10,000 units with as little as $25.

CARRY TRADE EXAMPLE

Let's work with a 100:1 leverage. Many brokers offer 200:1, 400:1 or even 500:1 leverage, but keep in mind that leverage can also work against you; it is the ultimate double-edged sword.

A popular carry trade on the forex is the one involving the Japanese yen. The Japanese central bank (Bank of Japan, BOJ) has kept the interest rate at historic lows since the middle of the 1990s, to buy time against the rising yen and stimulate the export industry (which desperately needs a cheap yen to stay competitive abroad).

Forex traders wanting to set up a carry trade therefore often sell the yen – with an interest rate at 0,10% – and buy the Australian Dollar – with an interest rate at 3,75%. The interest rate difference of 3,65% is the positive carry.

Suppose you want to put $1,000 in this carry trade, using a leverage of 100:1. That means you would control $100,000 in currency with your $1,000. Let's say you keep this position open for a year. To be clear, you're not buying this position to speculate on the AUD/JPY per se, but to get a high Return On Investment, or ROI (your $1,000) by profiting from the interest rate difference between the Japanese Yen and the Australian Dollar.

Three things could happen:

1. **The position declines in value**. That damn yen keeps rising and rising, which is something the Japanese won't like any more than you do. After a while it triggers your stop loss, kicking you out of the trade before you can say sayonara to your $1,000 (committing ritualized harakiri is optional)
2. **Nothing much happens** with the value of the AUD/JPY. It goes up a little bit, down a little bit, but at the end of the year the rate is pretty much where it was when you opened the position. This is a definite possibility, especially when working with a stop loss of a 1,000 pips. In this case, you wouldn't make anything on the position itself, but the $1,000 will have yielded you 3,65% in interest over $100,000, equal to 365% interest over the $1,000 you actually put up yourself. Not bad at all!

3. **The position gains in value**. Obviously the best case scenario. Perhaps the Japanese central bank has flushed the Japanese monetary system with more cheap money or threatened to do so, pushing the yen down. At any rate, you will have made 365% interest on your $1,000, in addition to whatever amount of pips your position has improved in value. Yummy!

HOW TO SPOT A GOOD CARRY TRADE

Two things are important for spotting a good carry trade. First, you have to find two currencies with a big difference in interest rates. Secondly, the currency pair of those currencies should be clearly trending in the direction you need for your carry trade – meaning the currency with the higher interest should be on the rise.

Check out the daily chart of the AUD/JPY, and remember that the interest rate difference between the Aussie and the Yen is 3,65%, in favor of the Australian dollar. Since the beginning of 2009 the Australian Dollar has been in a clear uptrend, which makes it ideal for a carry trade with the AUD as the currency to buy.

AUD/JPY 2009-2011

SUMMARY OF THE CARRY TRADE

The carry trade can be a very lucrative strategy under the right circumstances. The most important conditions a good carry trade has to meet are:

1. A stable economic market, where the relation between the two currencies involved is relatively clear.

2. A sizable interest rate difference between both currencies, preferably more than 3%
3. A clear, long term uptrend for the currency that will be bought (the one with the higher interest rate)

Invest only a small part of your trading capital in carry trades, no more than a couple percent. It can be somewhat higher than what you put in a short-term trade though, because you want to keep the position open for a longer period of time and therefore need to give it a little breathing room.

Chapter 21 Trading the News

The forex is the domain of (intra) day traders more than any other financial market. Many positions are opened and closed within one trading session. Because there are so many highly active traders on the forex, important and or unexpected (economic) news can easily cause violent market swings.

A well known example is the monthly publication of the American employment figures, also known as the *non-farm payrolls*. Price development of the majors (the five most important currency pairs, which all have the US Dollar in them) can be very volatile right before – and especially right after – the publication of these figures.

Trading important economic news like this is exciting, fun and potentially very profitable, but can just as easily result in quick losses when treated lightly.

How to Trade the News

Sometimes, important economic news has a long-term impact on the price development of a currency pair. It could even be the catalyst for a real life trend reversal, but in most cases the direct, noticeable effect of economic news events has a limited life span, of 60 to 90 minutes. After that, prices will often slowly retrace to the level they were trading at before the news was published.

Does that mean important news normally has no effect at all after those 90 minutes? No, but the direct impact on the forex will subside most of the time. After that, it will be just one of many factors traders take into account when deciding upon entering or exiting the market.

Trading the News

5 *Minute Charts*

Because we're looking at a window of only 90 minutes and are therefore going for a trade with a very short life span, we will be using 5 minute candlestick charts for the currency pair we are targeting. We will be looking for a clear signal on that chart within that time frame, just after the news has been published.

Difference between Actual and Expected Figures

Usually, the further the actual numbers are from the expected numbers, the more extreme the market's reaction. This makes sense of course. When the expectation is that the non-farms have increased by 100k and that expectation turns out to be correct, much of the news will have already been 'priced in'. This decreases the chance there will be much of a reaction on the news event.

Which Direction Is Not Important

Although the direction of the price development might seem obvious given the outcome of the news event, it doesn't always pan out that way. Therefore you should not bank on it too heavily. It might be logical to expect that the US Dollar will firm up when the non-farm employment figures have unexpectedly risen much more than expected, but that is still no guarantee that it will. Yes, rising employment rates are good for the economy, which in turn is good for the dollar. However, traders might be worried about the high US national debt, causing a lukewarm reaction to the positive non-farms surprise. Subsequently, that lukewarm reaction makes traders realize that there is greater downside risk for the dollar than there is upside potential, causing everybody to short the dollar. Result: the dollar falls despite good employment figures.

Clear Direction IS Important

At the end of the day, as a trader, you don't care whether prices go up or down, as long as you are on the right side of the trade. We are therefore primarily looking for a clear reaction to the news event, not a logical one.

Take a look at the 5 minute candlestick chart for the EUR/USD at the time of a non-farm publication. After the figures have been published, we're waiting for the closing of the first two candles. Only when they both close in the same direction would we enter the market.

Tight Stops

Because we are looking for a clear direction we can use tight stops. Should the price retrace, we will be stopped out quickly; and although that would be a shame of course, it also limits our exposure. The set-up is based on the supposition that the price develops in a clear direction following the news event (as we have stated before, **which** direction is irrelevant). When the direction of the price turns out to be unclear after all, it's better to exit the trade.

Trailing Stops

The idea with a trade like this is of course to catch as much as possible of the temporary rally, but because it's difficult to predict how far it can push on, putting in a profit target isn't the best method here.

As said, we initially put the stop close to the entry point, but as the trade starts to move in our direction, it's recommended to lock in at least part of the profit. There are basically two ways to do this, either by using a *trailing stop*, or by manually moving your stop. A trailing stop is a stop that automatically moves with the position, at a pre-determined distance (something like 30 pips for instance). Then, when the price moves 30 pips in your direction, the stop would automatically move to your break even point. In case of a strong rally a trailing stop can thus let you ride the entire wave, without being pushed out because of a profit target or risk losing everything if prices eventually retrace. Of course you could also opt to move your stop manually, but that introduces a psychological element to the trade that not everybody can handle. (how cool are you really in the face of greed and fear?)

Summary

Trading the news can turn quick profits, but is also prone to risks. It's therefore important to wait for a clear direction (whether up or down is irrelevant) and place tight stops, in order to decrease your risk exposure. Don't put in a profit target and let your stops move with the position – preferably through a trailing stop – when the trade goes your way.

PART V

How to Become a Successful Forex Trader

Knowing what drives the forex is important, just as having a good trading strategy is, but these are still not the most important conditions for success as a forex trader. Trading on a financial market (or, more accurately, speculating) is first of all playing a psychological game with yourself, and only secondly against others (i.e. 'the market')

The currency market is the Wild West of the financial world. There are few rules, a lot of players both big and small, riches for the taking, lots of risk, winners, losers and a buffet of unpredictable dynamics. The current, fast growing popularity of the forex certainly has similarities with the gold rush at the beginning of the last century, when everybody and their grandmother headed into the mountains in search for their *Sierra Madre* moment.

For most of these prospectors (and their grandmothers) the adventures ended in disappointment. Why? Because they lacked one or several of the necessary ingredients: preparation, willingness to work hard, stamina, discipline, self-knowledge and (a little bit of) luck.

Chapter 22 What Kind of Trading Is Right for You

Goals

Every project starts with the formulation of goals, targets and ambitions. This process is a goal in its own right, because it forces you to think about the possibilities and limitations of the project, given the time and money you're able and or willing to commit. Based on those investments you will then think up a strategy which enables you to reach your goals.

Your goals should first and foremost be realistic. Sounds logical, I know, but temptations born out of enthusiasm and inexperience can be strong and persuasive. It's a duo that often promises pots of gold before a rainbow has even appeared. So, even though enthusiasm is great, don't let it blind you.

One of the most obvious goals when it comes to trading the market is a financial goal, in combination with a specific time table. To be able to make a realistic estimate you should seriously consider the following parameters:

Time

How much time can you commit to trading the forex? Do you have a demanding job, which leaves you only half an hour at the beginning or end of the day to study the markets and open or close positions? Then intra-day trading is probably not for you. But if you are a student, odds are you can more easily spend a couple of hours a day getting rich on the forex, before graduating and having to start looking for a job.

Study

Increasing your knowledge about trading the currency market also takes time. It will be worth your while though, because the more you know, the more tools you'll have to perfect your trading system. You might discover that Fibonacci levels work for you; so you read a couple of books about it and learn how to use fib extensions with increasing success. Or your might discover range trading as an alternative way of trading to the trend trading you have been doing from the start. Adding range trading to your trading repertoire would enable you to put on profitable positions more often, simply because the market is ranging more often than it is trending.

Simply put, the more time you free up for learning about trading, the quicker you will develop as a trader, so you can perfect and expand your trading methods and improve your return on investment.

Money

Last but not least, money. Yes, it's possible to start with $300 and turn it into $10,000, but not in a couple of months. Your financial goals are therefore at least partly determined by your trading capital. Bear in mind that most of the time the smart money is on starting with a small investment and a modest financial goal. Many forex traders lose their first bankroll, which is why it's better to try and turn $300 into $1,000 than $10,000 into $30,000. After yo have reached the more modest goal, you can move up the target.

WHY MOST TRADERS LOSE MONEY

Trading on a dynamic market like the forex can be very emotional, which is never a good thing when trying to let your money work for you. Being successful as a forex trader is therefore more than simply having a good trading strategy. Everybody has his strengths and weaknesses, preferences and prejudices. Knowing yours will help you decide on the kind of market you want to trade in and how to be successful in that market.

Since it's obvious that anyone can learn to interpret charts, follow the news, buy low and sell high, it follows that trading the currency market in itself really should not be all that difficult, especially for those that are willing to invest time and effort into it. So why are so many traders losing money on the forex? Mostly because they fall in one (or all) of the following categories:

1. **The Gamblers**. These are the real idiots. They treat the market like a casino and expect to become rich overnight (or at least over a couple of nights). Being consistently profitable is impossible for this group, because they simply don't think anything through but instead operate on wishful thinking. They go short because they think the price should really start falling and long because they can't imagine prices going lower. They invest far too much of their trading capital in a single position, buy out of greed and sell in a panic.

2. **The Lost Boys**. These guys *do* think, but they lack structure, in other words a system. They have some understanding of how the market works, but still trade ad hoc most of the time. They don't monitor their Expected Value, regularly invest too much in a single position and learn only sparingly, because they lack a system that allows them to learn from their experiences.

3. **The Psychos**. They know how the market works and have solid trading systems. The only problem is they're not following them. They are a bit like those very normal, very nice people that turn into raving suicidal maniacs as soon as they get into a car; suddenly they are willing to risk life and limb just to be home 30 seconds sooner. Some psychos really can't help themselves (therapy might work) others really don't need to get themselves into trouble the way they do. They might have a trading strategy based on waiting patiently for the ideal long term trade, but they themselves are as impatient as little boys right before school gets out.

A good trading system is more than just a trading strategy, it's a collection of personal choices, delivering a tailor made *modus operandi*. Your trading strategy might be the engine, but you also have to make sure it's suitable for the particular car you are driving.

To get to a trading system that's tailored to your personality and situation in life, you should answer some questions for yourself, about your personal preferences, strengths, weaknesses and ideas about how markets function. At first sight this might seem like psychobabble, but in the end your trading system is somewhat like a company with only one person in it: you. Wouldn't you think it a good idea to do a little personality assessment of an employee when the success of the company depends entirely on that employee? Below are some questions that can help you set up a trading system suited to your personality and determine the amount of time and money you can invest in your budding forex career. And no, there are no wrong answers

SELF-ASSESSMENT

1. On a scale of 1 to 10, how much do you know about the financial markets?
2. How much time can you spend studying up?
3. How much time can you spend trading daily?
4. Are you someone that easily understands technical matters, or are you more of a people person?
5. Would you describe yourself as more disciplined, or more impulsive?
6. Would you consider yourself impatient?
7. What do you think your strong points are when it comes to trading?
8. And your weaknesses?
9. What do you think you should learn before seriously starting your trading career?
10. Do you like to be right?
11. What do you hope to achieve as a forex trader? Enough to pay for your annual vacation? A modest supplement to your income? A Ferrari, flying first class for the rest of your life, or simply a fat bank account?
12. How motivated are you to reach your financial goals?

13. Are you an optimist, a realist, a pessimist?
14. Would you be able to pull the plug on a losing trade ten times in a row for that one, very profitable trade, or would you rather have seven small profitable trades and three small losses?
15. Without thinking too long: would you rather trade short term or long term? And why?
16. Are you good at working alone?
17. Are you easily distracted? And if so, would this bother you when you're trading?
18. How much would you risk to reach your goal?
19. What kind of trading system would you prefer? A trend following system where you hold positions for a longer period of time? Range trading, looking for more short term price developments? Or intra-day, moving in and out of positions multiple times a day?
20. Would you rather trade a lot of different currency pairs or specialize in a couple of them, for instance just the *Majors*?
21. Do you like volatile markets, swinging back and forth, with lots of chances for quick profits (but also more risk of being stopped out)?
22. How do you think the markets function? Do you believe it's all random, are you into chart patterns, or do you think the market is mainly influenced by macro-economic news?
23. Do you prefer small stops, meaning being stopped out more often but with smaller losses? And would you be able to enter the market again when the price development looks to be moving into your direction after all, even after you've been stopped out in that exact position once or twice already?
24. How will you take profit? Are you the impulsive kind or do you prefer setting targets beforehand? And if you set profit targets, do you keep them?
25. How would you protect your trading capital? How would you prevent from going bust?

Of course this questionnaire is not the whole shebang. What you should take away from this is that it's important to take some time to ask yourself some serious questions, to find out what kind of trader you are. Where is your *edge* when it comes to trading the markets? What should you watch out for? What do you like and what do you hate? Are you disciplined enough, motivated enough, do you have enough time and money to reach the goals you have set yourself?

Answering these questions will in help you on your way to finding the trading system that is best suited for you.

Trader X

Below the example of a beginning trader, some of his answers to the self-assessment questions and his subsequent choice for a trading system. Just to give you some idea about the insights answering the above questions could give you.

Trader X has a lot of time and is highly motivated.

He thinks he is a quick study and has become very disciplined in his years as a professional poker player.

He has a somewhat impatient and impulsive personality.

Trader X is good at math.

Trader X thinks that his impulsive nature might prove problematic in trading

His initial goal is modest. He would like to prove to himself he's able to trade profitably and has therefore set himself an initial goal of increasing his $500 starting capital to $2,000 in six month's time. After reaching that goal he will decide on a new one.

He doesn't like to lose, but thinks he can handle it as long as the losses are small.

At first he liked the idea of long term trading a lot, but after reflecting on it a bit he realizes he probably won't have the patience for it.

He wouldn't mind losing his $500 trading capital that much, although he obviously hopes to avoid it.

Trader X is impartial to the direction of the market, as long as he doesn't have to stay in a position for too long.

He wants to concentrate on one or two currency pairs in the beginning, figuring that forex trading is complicated enough as it is.

He thinks that, to a certain extent, the market moves in patterns. He still has a lot to learn, but from what he can see it seems price developments do run into support and resistance levels and repeat themselves regularly.

He prefers small stops, to keep his losses small. He knows this means he will have to accept being stopped out a lot, but doesn't mind this that much. Should he be stopped out in a market that still looks interesting to enter, he could easily see himself get in again. But small stops give him a sense of control, which he likes.

When it comes to profit taking, he prefers choosing targets in advance, based on support and resistance levels. He thinks this is of particular importance, because his impulsiveness might otherwise tempt him into taking profit too soon.

He protects his trading capital by putting on small positions, so he can absorb a losing streak without losing everything.

Trading Conditions Trader X
* Bankroll $500.
* Short-term trading.
* EUR/USD and GBP/USD exclusively.
* How to decide to enter the market: look at patterns in price developments, to be discovered through technical indicators and the studying of candlestick charts.
* Tight stops, for a maximum of two percent of the total trading capital. This is still pretty aggressive, but trader X doesn't want to start out with a bigger trading capital.
* Profit targets based on support and resistance points. Because he is prone to impulsiveness and impatience, trader X will be particular strict about sticking to his profit targets.
* Position size is percentage based, in other words, two percent risk per trade.

The situation described here is obviously a short, short version, but hopefully it will give you some idea about how self-analysis can help you formulate a number of personalized trading conditions for your trading system. It's important to construct your system based on your strengths, while avoiding your weaknesses. However, you should give special attention to those parts of your trading system where you can't get around your weaknesses and work to strengthen them, in order to become more successful.

CHAPTER 23 SET-UPS

An important part of a profitable trading system is knowing when to open a position. This is where fundamental and technical analysis can be of help. Prices on the forex are the direct result of supply and demand, and both fundamentals and technicals can give insight into the eternal power struggle between the bulls – who are rooting for the uptrend – and the bears (the pessimists, so to speak). A set-up is a collection of fundamental and technical conditions that have to be met before a position is opened.

SET-UP EXAMPLE I: BOLLINGER BANDS BREAKOUT
1. Use of Bollinger Bands to put the significance of price developments in perspective.
2. The price has to break through the upper or lower band (breakout)
3. The candle has to close above the upper or below the lower band
4. Subsequently, the price has to retrace to below the upper band (in case of an uptrend) or above the lower band (in case of a downtrend)
5. Only when all of these conditions are met will a position be opened in the direction of the breakout.

SET-UP EXAMPLE II: SMA BREAKOUT

In the 1980s, a famous group of traders nicknamed *The Turtles* made a name for themselves trading the commodities market. It was a group of about 10 people that started out without any special knowledge about trading the markets, their professions ranging from postman to accountant. They were trained by a very successful commodities trader[26], who wanted to prove that anybody could be taught to trade the markets successfully. The Turtles made more than $100 million in just a couple of years, and one of their favorite set-ups was trading the 20 day high/low of a given commodity. This was a simple, but at the time highly effective set-up, whereby the breakout from the 20 SMA (Simple Moving Average) was the trigger for opening a position.

As you can see, a set-up does not have to be all that complicated. There are countless movies on YouTube of traders that have surrounded themselves with a buffet of technical indicators, ranging from RSI and Bollinger Bands to Fibonacci, SMA 20, SMA 200, Stochastics, MACD and beyond. Of course this all looks very professional, but looking professional is no prerequisite for being successful as a trader. On the contrary really. Stories about successful traders are almost never

---

26 The trader in question was Richard Dennis, who, in 1983, had bet his partner, William Eckhardt, that everyone could be taught to become a successful trader. That same year the movie Trading Places – with Eddie Murphy and Dan Aykroyd in the lead – came out, based on this very theme. Coincidence?

about how they use 20 different technical indicators for their set-ups. Most of the time, simplicity is king.

WHY USE A SET-UP

Most beginning forex traders lose money. Not because trading currencies is so hard, but because it looks so *easy*. A highly dynamic market, high leverage, just deposit a couple of hundred bucks and on the road to riches you are! Many amateur traders get stung by this assumption. They are persuaded that it is somehow very easy to make a killing on the forex, without learning too much about it or investing some real money. Due to this, they fail to put some research into the habits of successful traders, or even learn from their own mistakes.

Put simply, most traders just put in too little effort. They have surfed through some pages on the internet, learned a bit about technical indicators on YouTube and picked up something here or there about the impact of economic news on the currency market. Next, they grab a set-up from wherever – because some dude said it worked wonders for him – and 'Shazaamm!' let the money flow in!

Obviously that is a bit of a pipe dream. Having a good set-up certainly is important, but it's maybe 10 percent of what you need to become successful as a forex trader. In this respect, it might be interesting to point out that there are several examples of traders that have run simulations with so called *random entry systems*, and who have discovered that one can trade profitably with these kinds of set-ups. That's not to say trading with a good set-up won't be more successful than trading without one, just that it's not all-important, as some trading system vendors will have you believe.

A Good Set-Up Is Important for the Following Reasons:

1. It forces you to think about good entry points.
2. It keeps you out of the market when you don't really know what to do with the current price development. (Even so, many traders regularly bypass their own set-up conditions, getting them into trades they are unhappy with from the get go, causing them exit the trade too early or too late, move their stop loss etc. Don't do this yourself, stick to your plan)
3. A set-up provides a frame of reference for the market situation you are looking for. It shouldn't be something you took away from some website without giving it a second thought, but a collection of conditions you think should be in place before you would open a trade with confidence. It doesn't mean you have to come up with the set-up all on your own, as long as it's one you can subscribe to (which will make it easier to stay disciplined and keep your eye on the ball once the position is opened).

Naturally you can use several different set-ups. One for a market moving sideways for instance, since 80% of the time markets are not trending but move back and forth. Another set-up for a bull market, one for a bear market, maybe even different Set-upsset-ups for different currency pairs. You could develop a set-up for the USD/CAD for example, in which the oil price plays a prominent part – since Canada is the largest supplier of oil to the US[27] there is a strong correlation between the oil price and the value of the Canadian dollar. Or a set-up for the NZD/USD that looks at movements in the AUD/USD, because New Zealand's economy has a strong correlation with the Australian economy.

But again, even if you have the best collection of set-ups ever, know that they only constitute about 10% of what's necessary to be successful on the forex.

27   Source: US Energy Information Administrator, US Imports by Country of Origin.

CHAPTER 24 EXIT STRATEGY

Knowing when to get out is at least as important as knowing when to get in.

Experts – some real, most self-appointed – offer tips about 'undiscovered stock market gems', 'inevitable price rises' and 'must have commodities' all over the internet. Interestingly enough, 95 percent of these tips only offer entry points and most of them are about **buying** stocks, bonds, commodities , etc. That's because most people prefer to speculate on rising stocks and the 'experts' are happy to oblige. On top of that, institutional traders often have a buy & hold strategy and would like other traders to keep to the same strategy, because it creates stability. These are only a few of the reasons why exit strategies often receive less attention than they should.

INFAMOUS EXAMPLES OF THE LACK OF AN EXIT STRATEGY

The absence of a solid exit strategy has been the cause of extreme blunders both inside and outside the financial world. It seems to be the case that loss aversion is such a fundamental part of human nature that even very smart and experienced people are capable of making dumb decisions because of it. Let's look at some to illustrate the point.

Example 1 World vs. Credit Crisis

The credit crisis of 2008 sent financial sectors worldwide into a free fall. After the fall of Lehman Brothers almost all banks were in jeopardy, and over the course of just a couple of days the world discovered it really could not afford the demise of any more big banks. Capitalism's default Darwinian exit strategy of survival of the fittest no longer seemed possible for a banking sector that was at the hub of every other business sector. Without anyone noticing a new situation had emerged where tens – if not hundreds – of global banks turned out to be 'too big too fail'. It was the new *'get out of jail free'* card for some of the richest companies on earth. Capitalism's new exit strategy? Keep those companies afloat no matter what (in other words: no exit strategy at all).

Example 2 the US vs. the Rest

The US military doesn't like exit strategies. It would probably deny this (then again, maybe not) but looking at the invasion of Normandy in 1944, and the wars in Vietnam, Iraq and Afghanistan, you cannot help but think the US military is unable to stand the idea of retreat, even if it seems the smart thing to do. In Normandy the gamble paid off, though military experts argue that it was a close call. However, in the decades since, this no retreat policy didn't always pan out that well, at the expense of a lot of lives and treasure. Most of the time, Plan B for the US military seems to be simply doubling down, in hopes of turning the tide after all.

Example 3 Oil Price vs. Hedge Funds

The reasonably unexpected fall of the oil price in the summer of 2008 brought several hedge funds to the brink of bankruptcy – and some even over. The reason, according to analysts from the Financial Times (among others), was their strategy to buy more oil when prices were going down, instead of taking a loss on investments going sour. Doubling down when prices are falling has the advantage that the benchmark (the average purchase price) will also fall, but when the price decline continues, the losses could of course rise to gargantuan proportions.

EXIT STRATEGY TO LIMIT LOSSES: THE STOP LOSS

Like Matt Damon said in the poker film *Rounders*: "*You can't lose what you don't put in the middle.*" In trading as well as in poker, limiting your losses is just as important as optimizing your profits – perhaps even more important. Every trader has losing trades every once and awhile, and every dollar saved in a losing trade is worth just as much as a dollar earned in a profitable trade. It's therefore important to formulate an exit strategy *before* you open a position. Think about why you want to open the position and base your stop loss on the answer.

Example I

You are an intra-day trader and use two back to back, 15 minute candles, going in the same direction as your main trade trigger. The goal is to earn 40-80 pips, which is very doable during small, intra-day trends in the Majors. You're not a top & bottom picker, but instead like to get in on the trade when the price movement has been under way for a while. In small, intra-day trends, retracement is often limited, so there's a good chance of a clear move.

You set your stop loss based on retracement within similar intra-day trends, earlier in the day. You get those retracements from 5 minute candlestick charts. For instance, you might spot that during an earlier intra-day trend, there was a temporary retracement of two small candles of about 15 pips in total. After that, the intra-day trend re-established itself. Taking a cue from that situation, you put your stop loss at 20 pips. You reason that a small retracement is always possible, but that when it exceeds 20 pips, the chance that the intra-day trend is about to reverse rapidly increases. Mind that this is a very tight stop, but even if you are right only 50 percent of the time you would still make money, even if your winning trades would never exceed 40 pips in profit per trade.

Example II

You are a short-to medium term trader and usually keep your positions open for no longer than a week. During that week your goal is to catch part of a trend that had already been under way. You prefer going long – simply because you prefer rising prices and find it difficult to speculate on falling prices. Most of the time, you put on a position just after prices retraced a little. The retracement has to be over though, increasing your chances of success to hook on to the upward trend. Your profit targets are usually at 200 – 300 pips.

You prefer to put your stops just below the lowest point of the retracement. This is logical, because if the price turns again, going below the earlier retracement, there is a stronger chance that the trend is over and a period of ranging prices is setting in – followed perhaps by a trend reversal. In any case the situation would be too blurry to take sides. You know this set-up produces a winner about 30% of the time, and your stops are usually about 50 – 80 pips away. So, on average, you will lose 2x 65 = 130 pips and you will make about 250, for an average profit of 120 pips per three trades, or 40 pips per trade.

EXIT STRATEGY TO SECURE AND MAXIMIZE PROFITS

Because not every trade can be a winner, it's all the more important to make sure the winning ones are as profitable as possible. Or, as the saying goes: 'cut your losses and let your profits run'. Most traders know this rule, but acting on it often turns out to be harder than expected. Greed and fear take turns to make losses from losing trades even bigger (by keep adding to the position for instance) and profits from profitable trades smaller by closing them too quickly, out of fear of having to give back the winnings later on. One simple guard against such behavior is picking a profit target before you open the trade.

There are several different ways to put in a profit target. For instance, you could make it time dependent. Keep the position open for a pre-determined time, an hour, a day, a week or for however long you want to – depending on what kind of trader you are, intra-day, short, medium, long-term – before automatically closing it (assuming it's a winning trade that hasn't been stopped out already of course).

These kind of time targets have obvious limitations – one of them being they don't take current developments into account at all – but for some traders they're the best solution. If you always have the feeling you get out too soon or too late when working with price targets, then it can definitely be helpful to simply say: whatever happens, in 24 hours I will close this position.

Another choice, used by many successful traders, is to use a trailing stop as exit strategy, or to look at price targets.

They might chose support/resistance points that lie within the trading range of

146 - JELLE PETERS

their trading horizon. Suppose the EUR/USD is at 1,4750 and a long-term trader thinks the euro is going to rise in the longer term. He wouldn't mind keeping the position open for six months or more. Looking at the daily charts (1 candle = 1day) he observes that the EUR/USD has twice before touched the $1,6000 before falling back. He therefore puts his profit target at 1,60. He puts his stop a little below the low of the past 3 months, which is around 1,4500. So he will risk 250 pips to gain 1250. Whether or not that's a smart decision depends on the rest of his trading system. If he is right 20 percent of the time, it would cost him 1000 pips on average to gain 1250, for a profit of 50 pips per trade. That's not that much for a long term trader, but if he finds one such trade at least once a week and opens at least 1 Standard Contract (1 pip = $10) for each trade – when the oldest trade is six months old and would normally have reached its target – he would make $2,000 a month. That's certainly not enough to buy a new Ferrari every year, but a used Beamer is nice too.

SCALING EXIT POINTS

Many successful traders 'grow' in and out of their positions. They don't open the whole position at once, but start with only 1/3 position for example. The idea is that they want their hypothesis about price development to prove itself first, which is why they limit their risk to 1/3 of the total position. Should the price continue to move in their direction, they will open another third, followed by another third.

Conversely, you can also grow out of your position, using something referred to as *scaling exit points*. With scaling exit points, positions are closed separately and have different price targets. Below is an example of this. This is by no means the only way to use scaling exit points, it's simply an example of how you could use them to your advantage.

Example of scaling exit points

Trader X is an intra-day trader. He puts on two, long EUR/USD positions at $1,4750. He puts his stops at $1,4728.

- Position I – Entry $1,4750 – Target $1,4780
- Position II – Entry $1,4750 – Target $1,4820

At $1,4760 he puts on another long position, because he now has more evidence that the price is moving in his direction.

- Position III – Entry $1,4760 – Target $1,4900

When the price reaches $1,4780, position I is closed and trader X moves up the stop loss of position II to its break-even point, at $1,4750.

- At $1,4800 he moves the stop loss of position II and III to $1,4775.
- At $1,4820 the target of Position II is reached and the position is closed.

- At $1,4900 the third position is also closed.

If the trade goes well, trader X could pocket some nice profits. Moreover, he can lock in part of those profits early, by moving up his stop losses, without actually closing the positions. So if the move continues his profits will continue to accumulate. These different exit points are possible because trader X has divided his position in three parts. He can therefore realize profits for parts of his position without being out of the trade altogether.

How scaling exit points would best benefit your trading style is something you can find out by playing around with them a bit and spending some time thinking about it.

CHAPTER 25 MONEY MANAGEMENT

All profitable trading systems pay attention to money management. No matter how talented you are as a forex trader, if you don't follow any kind of money management you will eventually empty out your trading account.

Preemptively limiting your losses and deciding on some sort of exit strategy for profitable trades – as discussed in the previous chapter – is really only half the story when talking about how to protect your bankroll.

POSITION SIZING

In his excellent book with the worst title ever invented in the history of mankind (better that than the other way around) *Trade Your Way To Financial Freedom*[28], trader and psychologist Van K. Tharp writes about the importance of position sizing and expectancy (Expected Value). Tharp argues that what is generally considered to be money management is in itself an insufficient guarantee when it comes to protecting your trading capital. For instance, when you follow the rule of not risking more than 3 percent of your trading capital, you would be practicing money management, but it does not necessarily offer sufficient protection for your trading capital. Perhaps you're a long-term trader in a highly volatile market, stopped out 10 or 15 times in a row sometimes. Not everybody can stand losing 45 percent of his trading capital before one fat, juicy trade comes along to make it all right again. (aside from the question whether or not a trading system with a possible drawdown of 45 percent can even be considered a viable trading system). In other words, different personalities and trading strategies ask for different approaches.

Tharp approaches the idea of money management not passively but interactively. What kind of trader are you? In what kind of market are you active? How big is the *peak trough drawdown* (losing streak) that you could handle, psychologically speaking? How much money is your system making? Tharp takes the answers to these questions together to enable traders to create their own, optimal money management strategy. Needless to say this is far away from traditional money management.

Central to Tharp is *position sizing*, which he views in relation to the risk/reward ratio. There are several position sizing strategies, but the best one expresses position size as a percentage of total trading capital. It's important to realize that the size of the position is irrelevant here (it could be 100% of your total trading capital); what matters is the amount that is actually at risk. Generally speaking,Tharp considers three percent of total trading capital at risk to be aggressive, but it also depends on other factors of your trading system.

---

28   Trade Your Way To Financial Freedom, Van K. Tharp, McGraw-Hill, 1999.

For example, if you really can't stand losing trades and develop a profitable system that produces 90 percent winners (which is possible, but they will probably be small winners most of the time) and only small losing trades, it wouldn't be a problem to use position sizes where 5 percent of your trading capital is at risk. After all, your peak through drawdown would already be limited by the low percentage of losing trades.

The Most Important Goals of Position Sizing
1. Protecting your trading capital
2. Enabling you to determine your Expected Value (EV)
3. Enabling you to tweak your trading system, to optimize the expected value and minimize the risk of ruin.

Example

Trader Y has a trading system that produces about 50 percent winning trades. He is a short-term trader, has a forex mini account (1 pip = $1) and primarily focusses on trading the EUR/USD. He does not have much more information about his trading system yet, except that he has already lost half of his bankroll and has the feeling he's doing something wrong.

After a little research, he discovers that his profitable trades usually net him around 30 pips, while his losing trades cost him 60 pips – because he always puts his stop loss 60 pips away. He started out with a trading capital of $600, but now only $300 is left.

Trader Y's position size is therefore 10 percent (60 pips = $60 in a mini account) of his total trading capital. Or, more accurately, it used to be 10 percent, because now that his trading capital is down to $300, his position size of 60 pips per trade has actually risen to 20 percent of his total trading capital! Another 5 losing trades back to back – quite possible with a 50/50 system – and he will be broke.

There are several things wrong with Y's trading system.

His position size of 10 percent is much too big and aggressive, especially because of his 50/50 system. Everyone who has ever played or even watched a little roulette in the casino, knows it's not that uncommon for the little white ball to land on a red number ten times in a row, in which case Y would go broke.

Because trader Y doesn't adjust position size to his declining trading capital at all, his percentage of trading capital at risk continues to rise and is already up to 20 percent.

Apparently, trader Y doesn't look at his risk/reward ratio at all, because he is continuously risking 60 to win 30. You don't have to be a mathematical genius to realize this constitutes a negative expected value.

Protecting Your Trading Capital

One thing is certain, if you lose your trading capital you are out of the game, and if you can't trade anymore you could have the most awesome trading system in the world, but it sure as hell won't make you any money anymore.

So, do a little digging and find out how often you produce a winning trade as a percentage of total trades and adapt your position sizing (the percentage of total trading capital at risk per trade) accordingly. A good rule of thumb is to limit your position size to a maximum of 1/10 of the percentage of winning trades. For example, if you have a system that produces 50 percent winning trades, your maximum position size per trade should not be greater than 5 percent.

Keep in mind that you need to adjust your position size when your trading capital grows or shrinks substantially. It's not something you have to adjust after every trade – that would be too impractical – but after losing 25 percent of your trading capital it would be the smart thing to do to.

Expected Value (EV) and Calculating Your Evp

Minimizing risk of ruin and having a system with a positive Expected Value (+EV) is what it's all about when playing games that can be structurally profitable (at least for those who know how to play them).

As said, minimizing your risk of ruin can be achieved by connecting the percentage of winning trades to the height of your position size. If you are at the beginning of your trading career and really have no idea of the percentage of winning trades yet, a good starting point would be to assume 25 percent winning trades and a maximum position size of 2.5 percent per trade (meaning 2.5 percent of your total trading capital)

When trading the financial markets, Expected Value is a function of the percentage of winning trades, the average profit for winning trades, the average loss for losing trades and the position size.

Example
- You have a trading system that generates 40% winning trades.
- The average profit for those trades is 50 pips.
- Your position size is at most 4% of your total trading capital (1/10 of the percentage winning trades)
- Your total trading capital is $600, meaning your position size in dollars would be at most $24 per trade.

Over ten trades, the results – on average – would be as follows:
- 6 x -$24 = -$1444 x $50 = $200
- Total profit = $56
- Expected Value = $5,6

- EV expressed in position size (EVP) = 0.23

Expected Value expressed in position size (EVP) is nothing more than the Expected Value for each dollar you risk. An EVP of 0,23 therefore means that on average you make 23 dollar cent for each dollar you risk.

Expressing your EV in position size can be of use because it can you show you how your trading system is performing over a longer period of time, regardless of the (growing) size of your trading capital. Over time, absolute values change, but by expressing the EV in the value of the position size you can always see the relative result of your trading system. Generally speaking, the higher your EVP, the better your system is performing.

Conclusion

Many beginning traders don't have a trading system at all. They have not yet thought about what kind of trader they want to be (long-term, short-term, many small losses and a few big winners, or many small winners and few losing trades etc) or how to find out whether or not they're on the right track. Often, their analysis doesn't go much beyond "when my trading capital grows it's going well, when only 10 percent of my trading capital is left it's going badly".

This attitude/situation is understandable – when you've just discovered trading on the forex there are many things requiring your attention – but can also be costly. Developing a trading system is something that shouldn't be postponed until you're broke.

This chapter aims to show that it's important to start thinking about your trading system right away, to limit your risk, protect your trading capital and gain insight in the Expected Value per trade.

CHAPTER 26 SYSTEM EVALUATION

No matter how well your trading system performs, it can always do better. Especially in the beginning, it might not even do that well at all and you will be in need of a little help. To improve its performance, system evaluation can provide a critical view.

By now – If all goes well – you will have started developing a trading system suited to your personal situation, your strengths and your weaknesses; a system that uses multiple, solid set-ups, a fully thought through exit strategy and position sizing that protects your trading capital.

But you're never really finished with the job of developing a trading system. It will perpetually be under construction, like the *Sagrada Familia* in Barcelona; ever more beautiful, never finished. That's because everything around you also evolves and changes, just as you continue to evolve and develop as a person. Not only will you learn more as you go along, you'll also gain experience and might want to explore new markets, new strategies. Continuously testing your trading system is the only way to find out if new tactics, markets and strategies can contribute to your success as a trader. Simply keeping score by monitoring how your trading capital is doing won't be enough, because it doesn't answer the question about what is working and what is not.

THE NUMBERS

To get a good idea about the success of your trading system (or lack thereof) several figures can help you out, like EVP, trading capital growth/decline, *Total Percentage Winning Trades*.

Expected Value Expressed in Position Size (EVP)

The most important information you can get from your trading system is the average performance per trade. Of course, the more trades you've made, the more accurate this figure becomes. Chances are you will engage in a greater variety of trades over time. Range trading along side trend trading for example, or expanding beyond the Majors into a number of crosses, like the GBP/EUR and the EUR/JPY. Measuring the average result per different kind of trade can provide valuable information. Perhaps you'll find out that your results trading cross currency pairs are fairing far better than your trades in the Majors, something that would be hard to find out if you only looked at the changes of your trading capital as a whole.

EVP stands for *Expected Value expressed in position size* (see chapter 25 for a more in depth explanation). Based on the total percentage of winning trades you determine your position size in a specific market. The position size is the maximum percentage of the total trading capital that you are willing to risk per trade. Beginners are advised to start with a position size of no more than 2.5 percent. In other words, if you're a beginner and your trading capital totals $1,000, your position size should not be greater than $25 per trade.

Expected Value is the total net revenue divided by the total number of trades. So if you made $200 in 20 trades, your Expected Value (EV) would be $10 per trade.

Your EVP, or Expected value expressed in position size, would be 0.40 ($10 / $25) in this case. That means that for every dollar you risk, your average profit will be 40 dollar cent.

Trading Capital Growth/Decline

This number is not as important, because it gives you information about something you already know, namely how much is in your trading account. But many traders like keeping score of their trading activities through a solid figure, so there you have it.

It's best to keep track of your trading capital growth/decline on a monthly basis. You could plot these monthly results on a chart, giving you some idea about its development over time. Print out the chart and stick it on a wall at least 10 feet from your desk. If you can still see an upwarding trend on the chart while sitting at your desk, you can rest assured you're on the right track.

Percentage Total Winning Trades

This number is primarily important because it enables you to estimate your optimal position size. You could roughly keep to the following guidelines:
* 75 percent winning trades = 7.5 percent position size
* 50 percent winning trades = 5 percent position size
* 25 percent winning trades = 2.5 percent position size

Remember these are maximum position sizes, meaning the maximum position size should always be 1/10 of the total percentage winning trades.

WHAT TO EVALUATE AND HOW OFTEN

It's important to evaluate both the separate parts of your trading system as well as the system as a whole. Some parts are best evaluated once a month, while others need only an annual or bi-annual evaluation. Bear in mind that these frequencies are somewhat dependent on how active you are as a trader. If you put on only two trades a week for example, monthly evaluation will not give you any statistically relevant information.

Evaluation of Your Trading System in Numbers

If you are a day trader, the percentage of winning trades, your EVP and your trading capital growth/decline are best evaluated once a month. Many beginning traders are tempted to evaluate more often, but that will not gain you much additional insight (except into how easy it is to develop a compulsive obsessive disorder). Really, it's better to spend 29 days of the month on getting good results and only one day on evaluating them.

Evaluating Different Parts of Your Trading System

Going through the self-assessment once a month might be a little bit too much, but it does make sense to at least go through your strengths and weaknesses once a month as a beginning trader, and evaluate how you dealt with them in your trading. Especially for short-term traders there is considerable risk of big losses due to a few moments of weakness (or to a lack of focus on the kind of trades that play to your strengths).

The monthly evaluation of your set-up(s) is a must (again though, the frequency is also somewhat dependent on how active you are as a trader). Which set-ups performed best (and why) and which ones performed worst? Check out their EVP's to gain quick insight. Your exit strategy and position sizing should also be given a closer look at least once a month. You learn as you go along, so it's very possible – even likely – that these evaluations will lead to important adjustments.

TRADING LOG

Most trading platforms automatically keep a trading log for you. They show when you opened a trade, for which currency pair, if the position was long/short, the lot size, and what the result was.

It is still smart to keep your own trading log though. Not only because it allows you to add a little more detail about each trade – for instance about the set-up and the specific trigger that opened the position – but also because it makes you more conscious about the reasons for opening the position.

Example of a trading log
- Long EUR/USD 1,4755
- Stop/loss: 1,4738 (swing low for intra-day range is 1,4742)
- Target 1: 1,4780 (weak resistance level)
- Target 2: 1,4810 (strong resistance level)
- Reason: possible breakout intra-day range
- Result...

This is not the only possible way of keeping a trading log, you might want to add more information, or less, or different information. The point is to show that keeping a trading log yourself can give you more information than automated logs, which in turn could help you evaluate your trading system more specifically.

CHAPTER 27 THE PSYCHOLOGY OF TRADING

The difference between winning and losing is often razor thin. In life and sports as well as in trading the financial markets. How many legendary tennis matches have been decided by a difference of just a couple of points? How many soccer matches by a single, dangerous moment, sometimes completely against the odds?

Trading is no different. You will have losing trades, everybody does. The difference between profitable traders and losing traders often resides in those couple of losing trades that could have been prevented, that winning trade you shouldn't have missed, the profit target that was too soft, the stop loss that was too far away.

The more technically oriented traders are prone to say emotion doesn't play any part in their trading. After all, they have a trading system that is based on technical indicators, they have set-ups, stops, an exit strategy; everything is locked in from the beginning. There's no room left for emotion.

And yet, at the end of the day you are the one setting the parameters for that fully automated system. You can change the system, or chose to use another system. What would you do when your system loses 35 percent of your trading capital in just a short while? What if it all of a sudden puts on a losing trade ten times in a row? Would your adjustments of the automated trading system be just as automatic? Or might they be influenced by your emotions, if only a little bit?

Building a good defense starts with acknowledging the threat. Perhaps you are indeed less likely than others to make emotional decisions, but not taking into account something that is a known risk factor to almost everybody, seems a bit too nonchalant.

There are big and small reasons to NOT trade on the financial markets. Below are some of the most important ones.

WHEN YOU SHOULD NOT TRADE
1. When you don't really have the time to make a good decision. Those are the moments you're in danger of treating your set-ups the way some people treat pieces of a puzzle that don't fit; by ramming it in. It might look ok at first, but almost never ends well.
2. When you are tired, drunk or worse. You might have all the time of the world, but unfortunately you temporarily lack the brain power.

3. When you're an intuitive trader. Perhaps you have an especially good feel for price developments when studying charts and important economic news, only are not feeling 'it' today or this week. Don't worry, just take a couple of days off and don't trade.
4. When recently sustained losses are bothering you.
5. When you lack focus, for whatever reason.

WHEN YOU SHOULDN'T TRADE A LITTLE WHILE LONGER
1. When you have just started in a new job.
2. When you have just had a baby.
3. When you have just broken up with someone and are still busted up about it.
4. When you are out of sorts, even though you don't (yet) know why.
5. When you have financial worries.

WORST CASE SCENARIO STRATEGY

Nobody wants to think about disaster and when you're just starting out as a trader with a small trading capital you don't have to spend too much time on this part of your trading system yet. However, at some point you will be dealing with a much larger trading capital and will have to put some thought in it (preferably before a worst case scenario becomes reality and wipes you out).

The reason is obvious: a worst case scenario is by definition a disaster. Therefore, if you never mentally prepared for it, it will hit you harder and take you longer to bounce back.

Worst case scenario examples

Below are a couple of possible scenarios. Not all of them are just as likely, the point is to spend some time thinking about situations that might make trading difficult, if not impossible.

Situation 1: Dramatic Losses

You've already been successfully trading the forex for a while. You have increased your initial trading capital of $500 to about $10,000, in a little over a year. Suddenly, over the course of two months, you suffer considerable losses. Nothing seems to work anymore. You thought you had a good and solid system, but over the last two months you lost $6,000, a whopping 60 percent of your trading capital. Now what?

Situation 2: Girlfriend/Boyfriend Part I

Same as situation 1, only this time the reason for the drain on your trading capital is that your boyfriend or girlfriend – with whom you've been living for a couple of years – has just lost his or her job. On top of that your car broke down too. Your partner says there is no other choice than tapping your trading capital. What do you do?

Situation 3: No More Forex

What no one had thought would ever happen has happened: The Gold Standard is reinstated and all the major currencies are connected to gold once again. This means no more free floating currencies, effectively ending the forex.

Situation 4: Big Bad Government

The government has decided to discourage small, individual speculators from trading on the forex. Because forbidding it outright is not an option, a law is being implemented that will tax the first $50,000 in annual forex profits at 75 percent. You've have been doing nicely these past years, netting about $35,000 a year trading the forex. This law will effectively ruin you. What do you do?

Situation 5: Uptick Yourself

Due to the huge increase in speculative forex traders over the past couple of years, the United States and the EU have (in our hypothetical situation) decided more regulation is needed on the currency market. For this purpose the *Forex Lateral Overseeing Authority* (FLOAT) is created, which imposes an uptick rule on the forex. It's a rule that already exists on some stock markets and is thoroughly hated by speculative traders. It states that you can only go short after an uptick. In other words, you can only go short after the price has gone up at least a point. The result is that many traders are forced to remain on the sidelines when prices are falling fast and there is no retracement.

You are a forex scalper who prefers to go short – just as there are traders that prefer going long, you love falling prices – and will therefore be affected considerably by this. What do you do?

Situation 6: Girlfriend/Boyfriend Part II

You're totally hooked on trading. Not that you have 'a problem' or anything like that, because you rake in an average $30,000 a month. However, because you are glued to your four screens night after night, your girlfriend or boyfriend has totally had it. He or she gives you an ultimatum: either the candlesticks go, or they go. What do you do?

WORST CASE SCENARIO TIP FOR BEGINNING TRADERS

For a beginning trader there really is only one, true, worst case scenario -- losing your trading capital.

With an initial deposit of $500 or less, there is a reasonable chance this will happen. Even though you might feel terrible about it, bear in mind that Rome wasn't built in a day either. Becoming a successful trader takes time and at least some money. As a rule, this appears to be harder to accept for Europeans than for Americans, who seem more prepared to take on a little risk and get back on the horse again after they have fallen off.

That doesn't mean you should deposit another $500 right away after losing your first trading capital. On the contrary, it's probably best to take your foot of the gas for a while. Evaluate your trades and your trading system. Hopefully you've kept a trading log, but if not, most trading platforms offer a trading history for your trades and your trading system. No doubt you will discover a number of leaks – one of the predominant ones being not following one's own trading system. There will be adjustments to be made to help close those leaks.

Next, get back on the rocking horse (i.e. trading on your play money/demo account) before getting on that real life, kicking stallion that threw you off so brutally before. Keep reading, keep studying and keep practicing on your play money account with your changed and hopefully improved trading system. Thus building up your confidence to get back on that beautiful black stallion after a month or two. Because, honestly, what's more beautiful….

The End of the Beginning

Now that you have come this far – and I would not have expected any less from an ambitious beginner like yourself – you can feel a lot more confident about your ability to trade on the forex. You've learned about the fundamental factors influencing the forex, acquired background information on the most important currencies, learned about technical analysis and how to use some of the most important technical indicators. We have looked at popular trading strategies, at building your own trading system, money management and the psychology of trading.

From now on, you won't have any excuse for making mistakes having to do with poor money management, trading when you're not at the top of your game or using trading strategies that don't go well with your personality.

Of course this is not the end of your trading education. It is not even the beginning of the end. But perhaps it is the end of the beginning. (to paraphrase a legendary orator). For a list of other good forex books, information about forex brokers and questions you might have about this book or your forex strategy, check out www.forexforambitiousbeginners.com.

And now, for your final test, to see how much of all the new forex knowledge stuck with you, take the forex quiz!

PART VI
FOREX QUIZ

Below, you will find a quiz with 60 questions. They come from all parts of the book and range from very easy to very hard. The answers to the quiz are in the back of the book, as are the explanations. There's also a score card to give you some idea how well you did.

Questions about the quiz? Ask them at the forum of www.forexforambitiousbeginners.com. There will also be new forex problems added on the site on a regular basis.

About Part I How Does the Forex Market Work

QUESTION 1 WHAT IS THE SO CALLED 'GOLD STANDARD'?
A. The Family Crest of Louis the 14th, *Sun King* and first forex trader. His flag, 'The Gold Standard' was adopted as the unofficial flag of the forex.
B. Expressing a currency in a fixed weight in gold.
C. Expressing a currency in US Dollars.
D. 0,618, the magic number of the Fibonacci sequence.

QUESTION 2 WHICH CURRENCY IS CALLED 'THE' WORLD RESERVE CURRENCY?
A. The US Dollar.
B. The Euro.
C. The Chinese Yuan.
D. The SDR, the currency of the IMF, made up of the weighed average of the six most important currencies.

QUESTION 3 WHERE IS THE FOREX LOCATED?
A. Frankfurt.
B. London.
C. New York.
D. Nowhere.

QUESTION 4 WHEN IS THE FOREX OPEN?
A. 5 days a week, 12 hours a day.
B. 5 days a week, 24 hours a day.
C. Monday through Thursday, 24 hours a day.
D. Always.

QUESTION 5 WHO REGULATES THE FOREX?
A. The National Futures Association (NFA).
B. The Financial Services Authority (FSA).
C. The Marxist Redistribution Fund (MRF).
D. There is no central regulating authority for the forex.

QUESTION 6 YOU WANT TO SPECULATE ON THE RISE OF THE JAPANESE YEN AGAINST THE US DOLLAR. WHAT SHOULD YOU DO?

A. Go long the yen, meaning short the USD/JPY.
B. Go short the yen, meaning long the USD/JPY.
C. Go long the dollar.
D. Both A and C.

QUESTION 7 WHAT IS THE 'SPREAD'?

A. The original *Heinz Sandwich Spread*, often simply called 'The Spread'.
B. The difference between bid and ask price of a currency pair.
C. The difference between the stop loss and the profit target.
D. An erotic police film from the 1980s.

QUESTION 8 WHAT ARE CROSS CURRENCIES?

A. Currency pairs that do not have the US Dollar in them.
B. Currencies that are set up against each other.
C. Currencies that are set up against three other currencies.
D. Currencies from Christian countries, like the US Dollar and British Pound.

QUESTION 9 WHAT IS A PIP?

A. Two back to back losing trades.
B. The smallest measurable part of the price of a currency pair, often the fourth figure after the decimal point.
C. Slang for 'bankroll' among forex traders.
D. A price level a currency pair has trouble breaking through.

About Part II Trading on the Forex Yourself

QUESTION 10 WHAT IS A GOOD RULE OF THUMB FOR SOLID MONEY MANAGEMENT?

A. Never risk more than 10 percent of your trading capital.
B. Never risk more than 20 percent of your trading capital.
C. To have at least 10 times the trading capital needed to produce 1 winning trade on average.
D. To have at least 20 times the trading capital needed to produce 1 winning trade on average.

QUESTION 11 WHAT IS A REALISTIC RETURN ON INVESTMENT ON THE FOREX?

A. 35% annual return on investment.
B. Depends on your trading system.
C. 8%-10% annual return on investment.
D. An annual Ferrari, yacht and villa.

QUESTION 12 IS IT BEST TO START WITH A DEMO ACCOUNT OR A REAL ACCOUNT?
A. Demo account.
B. Real account.
C. Both.

About Part III Understanding and Predicting Price Movements

QUESTION 13 WHAT IS FUNDAMENTAL ANALYSIS?
A. Blowing yourself up in the middle of a populated square when others don't agree with your analysis.
B. Analysis based on fixed convictions.
C. Analyzing the forces that influence the economy, like production capacity, consumer confidence, unemployment, etc.
D. Studying price development in the past to help predict the future price development.

QUESTION 14 THE FEDERAL RESERVE (FED), ANNOUNCES IT IS RAISING THE INTEREST RATE BY 0,25%. THE RATE HIKE WAS NOT EXPECTED BY ANALYSTS. WHAT WILL PROBABLY HAPPEN TO THE DOLLAR NOW?
A. It will fall.
B. Nothing. The Federal interest rate has nothing to do with the development of the dollar.
C. Impossible to predict. In case of an unexpected rate hike, the chance of a rising dollar is about 50%.
D. It will rise.

QUESTION 15. IN HIS MONTHLY PRESS CONFERENCE, THE PRESIDENT OF THE ECB SAYS THE INFLATION IN THE EUROZONE CAME IN HIGHER THAN EXPECTED AT 2,8%. HE ADDS THAT THIS IS ABOVE THE INFLATION TARGET, WHICH LIES BETWEEN 0,5% AND 2%. WHAT DOES THIS MEAN, IF ANYTHING?
A. It's a sign the ECB might raise the interest rate soon. The euro will probably rise.
B. It's a sign the ECB might lower the interest rate soon. The euro will probably fall.
C. Inflation is not an important factor for ECB policy. It's therefore unlikely that anything will happen at all.
D. The ECB normally only acts when inflation is above 5% for a period of 12 months or longer. It's therefore unlikely that anything will happen at all.

QUESTION 16. THE JAPANESE FINANCE MINISTRY ANNOUNCES IT'S GOING TO STIMULATE THE ECONOMY BY PROVIDING MORE LIQUIDITY TO THE MONETARY SYSTEM. WILL THE YEN RISE OR FALL, AND WHY?

A. Fall, because the yen will be worth less when money is added to the monetary system.

B. Rise, because the yen will be worth more when money is added to the monetary system.

C. Fall, because traders will lose faith in the Japanese economy.

D. Rise, because traders expect the measure will succeed in stimulating the economy.

QUESTION 17 GERMAN EMPLOYMENT HAS UNEXPECTEDLY DECLINED. COULD THIS HAVE AN IMPACT ON THE PRICE DEVELOPMENT OF THE EURO?

A. No, Germany is only one of 12 nations that participate in the euro.

B. There is a 50/50 chance it will have an effect.

C. Yes, because the German economy is by far the biggest in the Eurozone.

D. No, employment figures have nothing to do with the forex.

QUESTION 18 EXISTING HOME SALES HAVE RISEN CONSIDERABLY IN THE UNITED STATES IN THE PAST MONTH. IS THAT GOOD OR BAD FOR THE DOLLAR?

A. Good. Increased home sales point to confidence in the economy. The economy is also stimulated by increased activity in home building and renovation.

B. Bad. When Americans sell their house it's usually because they have to relocate to a cheap motel.

C. Figures about existing home sales have no impact on the price development of the US dollar whatsoever.

D. Bad. To buy a house in the US you have to pay in dollars. The more dollars that are spent, the greater the chance the dollar will decline in value.

QUESTION 19 WHAT IS TECHNICAL ANALYSIS?

A. Analyzing the forces that impact the real economy, like production capacity, consumer confidence, employment data , etc.

B. Studying price developments in the past to help predict future price developments.

C. Studying trades from the past and basing predictions about your annual return on investment on them.

QUESTION 20 NAME THREE CANDLESTICK CHART PATTERNS

A. The Sake, the Teriyaki, and the Sashimi.

B. The Harakiri, the Banzai, and the Zero.

C. The Three White Soldiers, the Harami, and the Dark Cloud Cover.

QUESTION 21 WHAT OFTEN HAPPENS TO THE PRICE AFTER THE CHART SHOWS A DOUBLE TOP?
A. It declines, because it has become clear that there is not enough force in the rising trend.
B. It pushes through, because a price movement gets stronger from trying to break a resistance.
C. It hits the same top a third time.
D. Price development often slows down to moving only a couple of pips per hour.

QUESTION 22 WHAT OFTEN HAPPENS TO PRICE DEVELOPMENT AT THE END OF A HEAD AND SHOULDERS PATTERN?
A. It declines, because the second shoulder proves that the bulls are losing power.
B. It pushes through, because the second shoulder is a sign that the bulls are gathering strength for another attempt, which often succeeds.
C. Price development often describes a smiley figure after a head and shoulders pattern, by declining into a hammock like shape.
D. A head and shoulders pattern is often followed by a third shoulder.

QUESTION 23 WHAT IS A GOOD STRATEGY WHEN A SYMMETRICAL TRIANGLE IS FORMING?
A. Placing two entry orders, one slightly above the falling line of resistance and one slightly below the rising line of support.
B. Waiting for the breakout.
C. Placing a long order.
D. Placing a short order.

QUESTION 24 WHAT IS THE IDEA BEHIND THE CONCEPT OF SUPPORT & RESISTANCE?
A. That some price levels are harder to break than 'normal' price levels.
B. That certain numerical relationships that can be found in nature also impact price developments in the financial markets. The length of a trend is limited by those special numerical relationships, with the price level called 'resistance' on the upper side of the trend, and 'support' on its lower side.
C. Support and resistance are the two opposite Bollinger Bands.

QUESTION 25 THE SHORTER A CANDLESTICK CHART'S TIME FRAME, THE STRONGER ITS RESISTANCE & SUPPORT.
A. True.
B. False.

QUESTION 26 THE MORE OFTEN A SUPPORT/RESISTANCE LEVEL RESISTS AN ATTACK, THE STRONGER IT BECOMES.
A. True.
B. False.

QUESTION 27 WHAT IS A SIMPLE MOVING AVERAGE?
A. The sum of a certain number of closing prices, divided by that number.
B. The sum of a certain number of closing prices, divided by that number, giving more weight to more recent closing prices.
C. The average of the average prices.
D. An unreliable way of measuring the average price – hence the 'Simple'.

QUESTION 28 WHAT DOES IT MEAN WHEN THE PRICE IS ABOVE THE SMA?
A. That the price is in a downtrend.
B. That the price is in an uptrend.
C. It doesn't mean anything. (which is one of the reasons why it's considered an unreliable way of measuring)

QUESTION 29 WHAT ARE MOVING AVERAGE CROSSOVER SYSTEMS?
A. Set-ups based on situations where different MA's cross each other.
B. Moving Averages that are created by combining several Moving Averages which are crossing each other.
C. Trading systems based on Moving Averages that look a lot like Bollinger Bands, another technical indicator, hence the term 'Crossover'.

QUESTION 30 WHAT IS THE MAIN STRENGTH OF THE RELATIVE STRENGTH INDEX?
A. It filters out the noise of the market, because it shows the relative strength of a trend.
B. It shows the strength of a particular resistance/support level.
C. That you can use it as a range trading tool.
D. That it shows where retracement will likely take place.

QUESTION 31 WHAT IS THE USE OF THE FIBONACCI SEQUENCE IN FOREX TRADING BASED ON?
A. Nothing.
B. The formula $Fn = F(N-1) + F(n-2)$
C. The Golden Ratio.

About Part IV Forex Trading Strategies

QUESTION 32 PRICES ARE RANGING MORE OFTEN THAN THEY ARE TRENDING.
A. True.
B. False.

QUESTION 33 WHAT IS RETRACEMENT?
A. A technique whereby the trader tries to find out how his trading system has progressed.
B. The partial retreat of a price after a significant rise or decline.
C. A set-up that seeks to repeat or copy a trade with one currency pair on another currency pair.
D. The breakout of a price development.

QUESTION 34 WHY IS TREND TRADING NOT FOR EVERYBODY?
A. Because you need a hefty trading capital for it.
B. Because it's a fairly complex way of trading, too hard for beginners for example.
C. Because it's often very hard to recognize a trend.
D. Because it usually means accepting a lot of small losses to produce one big winner, and not everybody can take that.

QUESTION 35 WHEN IS THE BEST TIME TO RANGE TRADE?
A. When you have a lot of trading capital.
B. During the European session.
C. When the market is relatively calm.
D. Saturday.

QUESTION 36 THE MORE TWO CURRENCIES ARE MUTUALLY DEPENDENT, THE MORE THEIR CURRENCY PAIR WILL BE RANGING.
A. True.
B. False.

QUESTION 37 WHICH TECHNICAL INDICATOR WORKS BEST FOR RECOGNIZING A POSSIBLE RANGE TRADE?
A. RSI.
B. Exponential Moving Averages.
C. Simple Moving Averages.
D. Bollinger Bands.

QUESTION 38 WHAT SHOULD YOU NEVER DO AFTER SETTING UP A RANGE TRADE?
A. Chase the breakout when your stop loss is triggered.
B. Use stop losses that are too tight.
C. Lose sight of the actual price development.
D. Put on a trend trade with another currency pair.

QUESTION 39 WHAT IS SCALPING?
A. The tradition among forex traders to shave their heads if they have ended the year with a negative return on investment.
B. A strategy whereby the whole trading capital is deployed in a single trade and the position is closed as soon as the profit is double the spread.
C. Gradually 'growing' into a position, so as to limit the exposure risk.
D. Keeping positions open only for a very short period, in order to quickly pick up small profits.

QUESTION 40 IS SCALPING CONSIDERED A GOOD STRATEGY FOR BEGINNING TRADERS?
A. No, because it requires a lot of discipline and stress tolerance.
B. Yes, because it doesn't require an actual strategy, only good timing.
C. Yes, because only small amounts of money are involved.
D. No, because large amounts of money are involved.

QUESTION 41 WHAT IS BREAKOUT TRADING?
A. Starting out with a new trading system.
B. Opening a position just as the price breaks through a resistance/support level.
C. Opening a position in the middle of a trend reversal.
D. Trading without a pre-planned strategy.

QUESTION 42 WHAT IS BREAKOUT FADING?
A. Opening a position when the breakout seems to fail.
B. Opening a position when the breakout transforms into a normal, solid trend.
C. Opening a position when the breakout is over and the price has returned to the start of the breakout.
D. Closing a position that was based on a breakout.

QUESTION 43 BREAKOUT FADING IS PRIMARILY MEANT AS A LONG TERM STRATEGY.
A. True.
B. False.

QUESTION 44 HOW DOES THE CARRY TRADE WORK?
A. You buy a currency that carries a low interest and sell a currency that carries a high interest.
B. You sell a currency that carries a low interest and buy a currency that carries a low interest.

QUESTION 45 BELOW IS THE CANDLESTICK CHART FOR THE EUR/USD JUST AFTER THE NON-FARM PAYROLLS HAVE BEEN PUBLISHED, WHICH SHOW THAT EMPLOYMENT HAS RISEN MORE THAN EXPECTED. IS THIS A GOOD MOMENT TO GET IN ON THE EURO/USD?
A. Yes, there is a clear, falling trend.
B. No. Although the price is falling, the period is much too short to speak of a trend, making successful entry highly unpredictable.
C. It's never wise to put on positions during these kinds of events.
D. It's better to wait. Should the trend still be in place after an hour, it might be interesting to get in.

About Part V How to Become a Successful Forex Trader

QUESTION 46 WHY DO MOST BEGINNING TRADERS LOSE MONEY TRADING ON THE FOREX?
A. Because they don't have a trading plan.
B. Because they lack realistic expectations.
C. Because they are unwilling to invest time and money.
D. All of the above.

QUESTION 47 IS SELF-ASSESSMENT IMPORTANT WHEN YOU WANT TO LEARN TO TRADE?
A. No, not when you have a solid trading strategy.
B. Yes, to find out what kind of trading system suits you best.
C. Not when you plan to use automated trading systems.

QUESTION 48 WHAT IS A SET-UP?
A. A set of conditions that has to be met before a position is opened.
B. Every trading strategy that uses Bollinger Bands.
C. A trade that turns against you just before it touches your profit target.
D. A trade with a tight profit target.

QUESTION 49 WHAT IS MORE IMPORTANT, A GOOD EXIT STRATEGY OR A GOOD ENTRY STRATEGY?
A. They are both equally important.
B. A good exit strategy.
C. A good entry strategy.

QUESTION 50 POSITION SIZING HAS NOTHING TO DO WITH RISK/REWARD RATIO.
A. True.
B. False.

QUESTION 51 WHAT IS ONE OF THE MOST IMPORTANT GOALS OF POSITION SIZING?
A. Maximizing profits.
B. Minimizing the risk of ruin.
C. To put on as many trades at the same time as possible.
D. To make optimal use of your trading capital.

QUESTION 52 TRADER X HAS $500 IN TRADING CAPITAL AND RISKS $75 PER TRADE. HE JUST STARTED TRADING ON THE FOREX AND EXPECTS THAT HIS TRADING STRATEGY WILL PRODUCE A WINNING TRADE 60% OF THE TIME. CALCULATE HIS POSITION SIZE AND DECIDE IF IT IS ADEQUATE OR TOO RISKY.
A. Position size is 15%, but this is too risky, it should be 6%.
B. Position size is 15%, which is about the correct position size.
C. Position size is 6%, which is about the correct position size.
D. There's not enough data to calculate the position size.

QUESTION 53 WHEN A TRADER HAS AN EXPECTED VALUE OF $5,6 PER OPEN POSITION AND RISKS $24 PER POSITION, WHAT WOULD BE HIS EXPECTED VALUE EXPRESSED IN POSITION SIZE (EVP)?
A. $5,6.
B. 23 dollar cent.

C.   46 dollar cent.
D.   There is not enough data to calculate the position size.

QUESTION 54 A GOOD RULE OF THUMB FOR THE MAXIMUM POSITION SIZE IS:
A.   1/5 of the total trading capital.
B.   1/10 of the total trading capital.
C.   1/10 of the total percentage of winning trades.
D.   1/100 of your total trading capital.

QUESTION 55 ARE THERE SITUATIONS WHEN YOU SHOULD NOT BE TRADING?
A.   There are several situations when you shouldn't be trading.
B.   Yes, for beginning traders there are, but experienced traders should be able to trade under all circumstances.
C.   That depends on your trading system.

QUESTION 56 IT IS NOT ALL THAT IMPORTANT TO READ FOREX BOOKS AND ARTICLES, AND PRACTICE A LOT, BECAUSE THE BEST FOREX TRADERS – THOSE UNDER 30 THAT HAVE ALREADY MADE MILLIONS FROM TRADING FOREX ONLINE – ARE PRIMARILY TRADING ON INSTINCT.
A.   False.
B.   True.
C.   Maybe.

QUESTION 57 A SUCCESSFUL TRADER CAN CLOSE EVERY TRADE WITH A PROFIT.
A.   True.
B.   False.

Bonus Questions

QUESTION 58 YOU ARE A BEGINNING TRADER AND HAVE PUT ON A POSITION TO SPECULATE ON THE EURO GOING HIGHER. YOU HAVE SET YOUR STOP LOSS AT 30 PIPS. AFTER ABOUT HALF AN HOUR THE TRADE IS VERY CLOSE TO YOUR STOP LOSS, BUT YOU HAVE A FEELING THE PRICE WILL STILL MAKE A TURN FOR THE BETTER. WHAT DO YOU DO?
A.   A successful trader trades on instinct. Listen to your gut and move that stop loss down to give the trade more room.
B.   See if there are news events supporting your gut feeling. If so, move up the stop loss. If not, only move the stop loss if your gut feeling is unchanged.
C.   Nothing.
D.   Open a second trade, with the same target as the first. Leave the stop loss of the first trade unchanged.

QUESTION 59 YOU ARE A DAY TRADER AND ARE HAVING A ROUGH DAY. YOU OPENED SIX TRADES EARLIER AND ALL SIX HAVE BEEN STOPPED OUT. YOU ARE PRETTY FRUSTRATED. WHAT DO YOU DO?

A.   Man up and open up six new trades.
B.   Man up, open six new trades and give them more room to breathe than the last six trades (put your stop loss further away)
C.   Call it quits for today.

QUESTION 60. YOU ARE A DAY TRADER. AN HOUR AGO YOU OPENED A POSITION BASED ON SOLID ANALYSIS, BUT NOTHING MUCH HAS HAPPENED SO FAR. THE PRICE WENT UP A LITTLE, DOWN A LITTLE, UP A LITTLE AGAIN , ETC. NEITHER YOUR STOP LOSS, NOR YOUR PROFIT TARGET HAVE COME EVEN CLOSE. WHAT DO YOU DO?

A.   Close the position and call it quits for today.
B.   Nothing.
C.   Close the position and go look for greener pastures.

APPENDIX I

ANSWERS QUIZ

1	B	21	A	41	B
2	A	22	A	42	C
3	D	23	A	43	B
4	B	24	A	44	B
5	D	25	B	45	A
6	A	26	A	46	D
7	B	27	A	47	B
8	A	28	B	48	A
9	B	29	A	49	B
10	C	30	A	50	B
11	B	31	A	51	B
12	C	32	A	52	A
13	C	33	B	53	B
14	D	34	D	54	C
15	A	35	C	55	A
16	A	36	A	56	A
17	C	37	D	57	B
18	A	38	A	58	C
19	B	39	D	59	C
20	C	40	A	60	B

APPENDIX II

Explanation
Answers Forex Quiz

Below are the answers and explanations to the quiz. Still left with questions? Go to www.forexforambitiousbeginners.com

About Part I How Does the Forex Market Work

QUESTION 1 WHAT IS THE SO CALLED 'GOLD STANDARD'?
A. *The Family Crest of Louis the 14th, Sun King and first forex trader. His flag, 'The Gold Standard' was adopted as the unofficial flag of the forex.* Really, you need an explanation on this one?
B. *Expressing a currency in a fixed weight in gold.* **This is the correct answer. The Gold Standard is a system that was implemented in many countries throughout the Nineteenth Century. It guaranteed the exchange of currency for a fixed amount of gold by the government. The Gold Standard proved hard to maintain, because it made monetary policy virtual impossible. Aside from the United States, all countries left the Gold Standard during WO I. The US followed in 1933, because of the Great Depression.**
C. *Expressing a currency in US Dollars.* In 1944, the Western allies decide in Bretton Woods that the US dollar will be fixed to the Gold Standard again, while the currencies of the other countries will be pegged to the US dollar, also known as the 'Gold Exchange Standard'. So, though answer C is incorrect, there has been a period when the currencies of many important countries were pegged to the US Dollar. The Gold Exchange Standard ended in the 1970s, when the US left the Gold Standard for the second time.
D. *0,618, the magic number of the Fibonacci sequence.* The number 0,618 is also known as the 'Golden Ratio', but not the Gold Standard.

QUESTION 2 WHICH CURRENCY IS CALLED 'THE' WORLD RESERVE CURRENCY?
A. *The US Dollar.* **The greenback is indeed still the most important currency in the world. All countries keep substantial dollar reserves, the five most important currency pairs all have the dollar in them and commodities such as gold, oil, gas and grain are all are priced in dollars.**
B. *The Euro.* The common currency of the European Monetary Union is more and more regarded as a reserve currency (even throughout the euro crisis) not the least because many countries want to decrease their exposure to the US dollar. However, quite apart from the euro crisis, the euro still has a long way to go if it wants to gain equal footing with the dollar.
C. *The Chinese Yuan.* The Yuan is definitely up and coming, but is not a part of the forex at the moment – it's not a free floating currency – neither is it part of the SDR (Special Drawing Rights) the currency unit of the IMF. China

would like to see the SDR as 'The' reserve currency and it might be in the future, but not as long as the Yuan is not freely exchangeable and/or a part of the SDR itself.

D. *The SDR, the currency of the IMF, made up of the weighed average of the six most important currencies.* As said, it's possible that this artificial currency will become the world's de facto reserve currency in the future, but it certainly is not as of today.

QUESTION 3 WHERE IS THE FOREX LOCATED?

A. *Frankfurt.* There is no central exchange for the forex, therefore D is the right answer, but Frankfurt is nevertheless a major financial center. The European Central Bank has its headquarters there.

B. *London.* Another important financial center.

C. *New York.* Important financial center, but not forex's HQ.

D. *Nowhere.* **Correct. In reality, 'The' forex doesn't exist. It's really just a network of banks dealing with each other in foreign currencies through Electronic Brokering Services (EBS) and Reuters Dealing 3000. There is no Wall Street address, no central authority, no limit in opening hours other than the opening hours banks around the world keep to. That's also the reason the forex is only closed during the weekend.**

QUESTION 4 WHEN IS THE FOREX OPEN?

A. *5 days a week, 12 hours a day.* Nope.

B. *5 days a week, 24 hours a day.* **Correct. This is because the opening hours of the forex are the same as those of banks. As long as there are banks open somewhere in the world, it's possible to trade. Thanks to the global time difference, there are banks open 24 hours a day, except over the weekend.**

C. *Monday through Thursday, 24 hours a day.* Banks are open Monday to Friday, not Monday to Thursday.

D. *Always.* You might expect the forex to always be open, especially since there is no brick and mortar exchange and everything is done electronically. But though the internet never closes, banks still do.

QUESTION 5 WHO REGULATES THE FOREX?

A. *The National Futures Association (NFA).* The NFA plays an important part in regulating US based forex brokers, but obviously not all the world's brokers are based in the US On the contrary, because of the stricter rules for US financial institutions, following the Dodd-Frank Act, many brokers left the US market.

B. *The Financial Services Authority (FSA).* The financial watchdog of the United Kingdom. Definitely important, because of London's importance as a financial hub, but not 'the' regulating authority when it comes to forex.

C. *The Marxist Redistribution Fund (MRF).* Ehmm, yeah, no of course not. (Disclaimer: any similarity between this fictitious organization and a possible existing organization that is actually trying to redistribute funds in a Marxist way, is accidental)

D. *There is no central regulating authority for the forex.* **Indeed there is not.**

QUESTION 6 YOU WANT TO SPECULATE ON THE RISE OF THE JAPANESE YEN AGAINST THE US DOLLAR. WHAT SHOULD YOU DO?

A. *Go long the yen, meaning short the USD/JPY.* **That is correct. Buying a currency is also known as going long, while selling is called going short. When you think the Yen will rise against the US dollar, you would go short the USD/JPY, speculating you will soon get less Yen for 1 Dollar.**

B. *Go short the yen, meaning long the USD/JPY.* Unfortunately, it's exactly the other way around.

C. *Go long the dollar.* No, you go long the dollar when you think it's going up.

D. *Both A and C.* No, because C is incorrect.

QUESTION 7 WHAT IS THE 'SPREAD'?

A. *The original Heinz Sandwich Spread, often simply called 'The Spread'.* They would have loved this over at Heinz, but it's not the correct answer.

B. *The difference between bid and ask price of a currency pair.* **Correct. It's also how the broker earns his money, by charging you the difference between bid and ask.**

C. *The difference between the stop loss and the profit target.* No, this has nothing to do with it.

D. *An erotic police film from the 1980s.* Unfortunately no. (Disclaimer: for those who consider themselves experts on erotic police films from the 1980s: any similarity between the forex spread and the possibly existing erotic police movie titled 'Spread' is accidental)

QUESTION 8 WHAT ARE CROSS CURRENCIES?

A. *Currency pairs that don't have the US Dollar in them.* **Correct.**

B. *Currencies that are traded against each other.* All currencies are traded against each other on the forex.

C. *Currencies that are set up against three other currencies.* So far, no currency triplets have been born on the forex.

D. *Currencies from Christian countries, like the US Dollar and British Pound.* Come on, you didn't really pick this one, did you?

QUESTION 9 WHAT IS A PIP?

A. *Two back to back losing trades.* This is so common we don't even have a nickname for it, so no.

B. *The smallest measurable part of the price of a currency pair, often the fourth figure after the decimal point.* **Correct.**

C. *Slang for 'bankroll' among forex traders.* Would have been nice, but no.

D. *A price level a currency pair has trouble breaking through.* No, that's called resistance or support.

About Part II Trading on the Forex Yourself

QUESTION 10 WHAT IS A GOOD RULE OF THUMB FOR SOLID MONEY MANAGEMENT?

A. *Never risk more than 10 percent of your trading capital.* No. Apart from the fact that this would be quite a lot, it also does not take into account what kind of trading system you are using.

B. *Never risk more than 20 percent of your trading capital.* This is even worse.

C. *To have at least 10 times the trading capital needed to produce 1 winning trade on average.* **Correct. This would sufficiently protect you against losing your entire trading capital, without being overprotective.**

D. *To have at least 20 times the trading capital needed to produce 1 winning trade on average.* This is a little bit too careful.

QUESTION 11 WHAT IS A REALISTIC RETURN ON INVESTMENT ON THE FOREX?

A. *35% annual return on investment.* This is a frequently asked question and although the 35 percent answer seems to be an internet favorite, it's not based on anything solid. The answer depends entirely on what kind of trader you are. If you're a scalper and start out with $1,000 in trading capital, an EV+ system and trade about 10 hours a day, it's entirely possible to grow your trading capital to $10,000 in less than a year.

B. *Depends on your trading system.* **Exactly.**

C. *8%-10% annual return on investment.* This is the kind of percentage commonly expected when investing conservatively in equities. It has nothing to do with trading the forex though.

D. *An annual Ferrari, yacht and villa.* Dependent on both your trading system and your trading capital. A successful forex trader with a working capital of $10 million might be able to put these things in his (or her) shopping cart at the annual millionaire's fair, but then again, most successful traders would rather use that money to make even more money next year!

QUESTION 12 IS IT BEST TO START WITH A DEMO ACCOUNT OR A REAL ACCOUNT?

A. *Demo account.* Seems to be the easy answer, but for most beginning traders it's not the best answer, because they trade very differently when there is actual, real money involved, as opposed to play money. A demo account is great to get to know a trading platform and/or test out a trading strategy, but being a great demo trader does not make you a great 'real' trader too.

B. *Real account.* Whether you're a beginning or more experienced trader, it is always sensible to have a demo account alongside to a real account, to test out new strategies and trading platforms.

C. *Both.* **This is simply the best answer.**

About Part III Understanding and Predicting Price Movements

QUESTION 13 WHAT IS FUNDAMENTAL ANALYSIS?

A. *Blowing yourself up in the middle of a populated square when others don't agree with your analysis.* This terrorist form of analysis has been out of fashion for a while on the forex.

B. *Analysis based on fixed convictions.* This would be the kind of fundamentalist analysis that has no basis in fact whatsoever and should be limited to Sundays (or Saturdays, if you wish, or Mondays, or Whateverdays)

C. *Analyzing the forces that influence the economy, like production capacity, consumer confidence, unemployment etc.* **The correct answer.**

D. *Studying price development in the past to help predict the future price development.* That would be the definition for technical analysis.

QUESTION 14 THE FEDERAL RESERVE (FED), ANNOUNCES IT IS RAISING THE INTEREST RATE BY 0,25%. THE RATE HIKE WAS NOT EXPECTED BY ANALYSTS. WHAT WILL PROBABLY HAPPEN TO THE DOLLAR NOW?

A. *It will fall.* If interest rates are being raised, it will be more expensive to borrow money (and more lucrative to lend it out). The value of the dollar will therefore most likely rise, especially since the interest raise was unexpected.

B. *Nothing.* The Federal interest rate has nothing to do with the development of the dollar. On the contrary, the interest rate policy of a central bank has everything to do with the price development of a currency.

C. *Impossible to predict. In case of an unexpected rate hike, the chance of a rising dollar is about 50%.* Incorrect, the chance of a rise in value is much higher (because credit will become more expensive), all the more when such a rise wasn't expected.

D. *It will rise.* **Correct.**

QUESTION 15. IN HIS MONTHLY PRESS CONFERENCE, THE PRESIDENT OF THE ECB SAYS THE INFLATION IN THE EUROZONE CAME IN HIGHER THAN EXPECTED AT 2,8%.

He Adds that This Is Above the Inflation Target, Which Lies Between 0,5% and 2%. What Does This Mean, If Anything?

A. *It's a sign the ECB might raise the interest rate soon. The euro will probably rise.* **Correct. Guarding price stability within the eurozone is one of the most important jobs of the European Central Bank. The ECB's inflation target lies between 0,5% and 2%. When it rises above 2% and the ECB signals it had not expected such an increase, there is a substantial chance the interest rate would be raised should inflation remain high. And a rate hike by the ECB usually means the euro will rise.**

B. *It is a sign the ECB might lower the interest rate soon. The euro will probably fall.* Actually, it's the other way around.

C. *Inflation is not an important factor for ECB policy. It's therefore unlikely that anything will happen at all.* On the contrary, the inflation figure is one of the most important factors influencing ECB policy, because guarding price stability is the ECB's first priority.

D. *The ECB normally only acts when inflation is above 5% for a period of 12 months or longer. It's therefore unlikely that anything will happen at all.* An inflation rate of 5% would be way too high for the ECB to accept for such a long period. The ECB would not wait 12 months before trying to do something about it.

Question 16. the Japanese Finance Ministry Announces it Is Going to Stimulate the Economy By Providing More Liquidity to the Monetary System. Will the Yen Rise or Fall, and Why?

A. *Fall, because the yen will be worth less when money is added to the monetary system.* **Correct. Stimulus programs like the buying of Japanese treasury bonds by the Japanese Central Bank (a practice also known as 'quantitative easing') increase the money supply. The more money there is available, the easier it is to get it. And the easier it is to get money, the lower the interest that can be charged for lending out money.**

B. *Rise, because the yen will be worth more when money is added to the monetary system.* That would be the world upside down. The more money you add to the system, the more expensive it gets? Think about Germany in the 1930s. Because of hyper-inflation, the Deutschmark had been reduced to rubble, raising the price of a sausage to 30 million Mark (and Germany produces a LOT of sausages, so they couldn't have been that expensive).

C. *Fall, because traders will lose faith in the Japanese economy.* When the government decides it's time to start stimulating the economy it is save to say that trust in the economy is already fairly low. Stimulating the economy with more money will therefore only be welcomed by investors. Confidence in the economy would therefore sooner increase than decrease.

D. *Rise, because traders expect the measure will succeed in stimulating the economy.* Of course it remains to be seen whether or not the economy will indeed start showing increased growth because of the announced measures. In the meantime the influx of new money will increase inflation, causing the price of the yen to decline compared to other currencies.

QUESTION 17 GERMAN EMPLOYMENT HAS UNEXPECTEDLY DECLINED. COULD THIS HAVE AN IMPACT ON THE PRICE DEVELOPMENT OF THE EURO?

A. *No, Germany is only one of 12 nations that participate in the euro.* Actually, there are 17 nations participating in the euro, but Germany is by far the most important member and its GDP makes up about 30% of the eurozone economy.

B. *There is a 50/50 chance it will have an effect.* Because the German economy is viewed as the engine of the Eurozone economy, the question whether or not falling German employment will have an impact on the euro is not a 50/50. The chance that the euro will fall due to rising German unemployment is much greater than that. Rising employment is often a sign of a weakening economy, and a weakened German economy might very well weaken other Euro economies.

C. *Yes, because the German economy is by far the biggest in the Eurozone.* **Correct**.

D. *No, employment figures have nothing to do with the forex.* Employment figures are among the most important economic figures for a currency. This is because employment directly influences consumer confidence and domestic consumption, while it also gives of a strong signal about the state of the private sector.

QUESTION 18 EXISTING HOME SALES HAVE RISEN CONSIDERABLY IN THE UNITED STATES IN THE PAST MONTH. IS THAT GOOD OR BAD FOR THE DOLLAR?

A. *Good. Increased home sales point to confidence in the economy. The economy is also stimulated by increased activity in home building and renovation.* **Correct**.

B. *Bad. When Americans sell their house it's usually because they have to relocate to a cheap motel.* Bull.

C. *Figures about existing home sales have no impact on the price development of the US dollar whatsoever.* Existing home sales are among the most important economic data when it comes to influencing the dollar

D. *Bad. To buy a house in the US you have to pay in dollars. The more dollars that are spent, the greater the chance the dollar will decline in value.* Spank yourself hard if this was your answer. (again, but harder).

QUESTION 19 WHAT IS TECHNICAL ANALYSIS?

A. *Analyzing the forces that impact the real economy, like production capacity,* consumer confidence, employment data , etc. Unfortunately, this is the definition for fundamental analysis.

B. *Studying price developments in the past to help predict future price developments.* **Correct. This studying of past price developments is usually done with the help of candlestick charts and technical indicators such as Bollinger Bands, RSI , etc.**

C. *Studying trades from the past and basing predictions about your annual return on investment on them.* Nope.

QUESTION 20 NAME THREE CANDLESTICK CHART PATTERNS

A. *The Sake, the Teriyaki, and the Sashimi.* "Waiter, can I have some more wasabi to go with my sushi?"

B. *The Harakiri, the Banzai, and the Zero.* If this really was your answer, you might like Seppuku as well.

C. *The Three White Soldiers, the Harami, and the Dark Cloud Cover.* **Yep, that's them, though, admittedly they could just as easily figure in a Japanese style Kama Sutra (if there is such a thing).**

QUESTION 21 WHAT OFTEN HAPPENS TO THE PRICE AFTER THE CHART SHOWS A DOUBLE TOP?

A. *It declines, because it has become clear that there is not enough force in the rising trend.* **Resistance and support levels often get stronger with each attack they repel. That makes sense, because more and more traders will base their entry- and exit strategy on those price levels, which have proven to be tough to break. In the case of the double top, it's entirely possible that the bulls will retreat for a while**

B. *It pushes through, because a price movement gets stronger from trying to break a resistance.* That doesn't make any sense; with each defeat it becomes harder to muster the strength needed to force another breakthrough, decreasing the chance of success.

C. *It hits the same top a third time.* Possibly, but in most cases, the price will not reach that same level a third time – at least not for a while.

D. *Price development often slows down to moving only a couple of pips per hour.* When the price stops moving, it means that the bulls and the bears are balanced out, something you would not expect after the bulls have just been pushed back twice in a row.

QUESTION 22 WHAT OFTEN HAPPENS TO PRICE DEVELOPMENT AT THE END OF A HEAD AND SHOULDERS PATTERN?

A. *It falls, because the second shoulder proves that the bulls are losing power.* **This situation is very similar to that of the double top. Although the bulls have raised their first top with a new high (the head), on the next try it** turns out the movement has lost strength (the second shoulder). It is now more likely that the price will decline, because the momentum is gone.

B. *It pushes through, because the second shoulder is a sign that the bulls are gathering strength for another attempt, which often succeeds.* This sounds a bit like the plot for Rocky (I to V). Very good fit for Hollywood, but less so for Wall Street.

C. *Price development often describes a smiley figure after a head and shoulders pattern, by declining into a hammock like shape.* Sounds quite nice but is total baloney.

D. *A head and shoulders pattern is often followed by a third shoulder.* This sometimes happens, but more often the price falls.

QUESTION 23 WHAT IS A GOOD STRATEGY WHEN A SYMMETRICAL TRIANGLE IS FORMING?

A. *Placing two entry orders, one slightly above the falling line of resistance and one slightly below the rising line of support.* **Correct. A symmetrical triangle often gives a clear signal that a breakout is imminent, but the direction of the breakout is unclear. To prevent missing part of the breakout move, you could place two stop orders, one for an upward breakout and one for a downward one.**

B. *Waiting for the breakout.* Also a possibility, but it would risk missing part of the breakout, which is why it's not the best solution here.

C. *Placing a long order.* Ok, but what if the breakout is heading the other direction? Because, as said, it's hard to predict which way the breakout will go.

D. *Placing a short order.* This creates the same problem as answer C.

QUESTION 24 WHAT IS THE IDEA BEHIND THE CONCEPT OF SUPPORT & RESISTANCE?

A. *That some price levels are harder to break than 'normal' price levels.* **Correct. This has everything to do with human behavior. For instance, nice round numbers often serve as resistance and support levels, as do price levels that have proven to be hard to break in the past.**

B. *That certain numerical relationships that can be found in nature also impact price developments in the financial markets.* The length of a trend is limited by those special numerical relationships, with the price level called 'resistance' on the upper side of the trend, and 'support' on its lower side. Has a nice ring to it, doesn't it? Still, it's baloney.

C. *Support and resistance are the two opposite Bollinger Bands.* The opposite Bollinger Bands are based on standard deviations of the actual, current prices. Although this has nothing to do with support & resistance, there is some correlation between the levels where resistance and support form and the upper and lower Bollinger Bands.

QUESTION 25 THE SHORTER A CANDLESTICK CHART'S TIME FRAME, THE STRONGER ITS RESISTANCE & SUPPORT.

A. *True*. Nope, it's the other way around. A resistance that formed 60 minutes ago on a 1 minute chart could easily be broken, whereas a resistance on a daily or weekly chart often has a lot more authority. It is also relevant for a lot more traders (since it wouldn't matter if you're a day trader or a long-term trader) while the resistance on a 1 minute chart is only relevant for intra-day traders.

B. **False**.

QUESTION 26 THE MORE OFTEN A SUPPORT/RESISTANCE LEVEL RESISTS AN ATTACK, THE STRONGER IT BECOMES.

A. *True*. **When a resistance or support level repels an attack, many traders will remember it the next time the price comes close to that resistance/support. Because of this, they are more likely to use the level as an entry point, profit target or stop loss, which will increase the importance of the resistance/support level even further.**

B. *False*.

QUESTION 27 WHAT IS A SIMPLE MOVING AVERAGE?

A. *The sum of a certain number of closing prices, divided by that number.* **Correct**.

B. *The sum of a certain number of closing prices, divided by that number, giving more weight to more recent closing prices.* No, that's the 'Exponential Moving Average' (EMA), thought up to decrease the lag caused by including prices from periods longer ago. By giving more weight to recent periods, an EMA has a better connection with current prices.

C. *The average of the average prices.* Nope.

D. *An unreliable way of measuring the average price – hence the 'Simple'.* The reason for adding the 'Simple' was because it only measures the average price over a specific number of periods. That's not so much unreliable as it is rough, especially in comparison to something like the Exponential Moving Average.

QUESTION 28 WHAT DOES IT MEAN WHEN THE PRICE IS ABOVE THE SMA?

A. *That the price is in a downtrend.* The SMA (Simple Moving Average) shows the average price over a certain period of time. Therefore, when the price is above the SMA, it means that the current price is higher than the average price. In other words, price development is currently in an uptrend, not a downtrend.

B. **That the price is in an uptrend.**

C. *It doesn't mean anything.* (which is one of the reasons why it's considered an unreliable way of measuring) The SMA is not an unreliable way of measuring price development, you just have to be careful about drawing conclusions from SMA lines alone – especially when it comes to the shorter period SMA's. It does mean something when the current price level is higher than that of the average price over a number of past periods, but whether it also means you should open a position depends on several other factors as well.

QUESTION 29 WHAT ARE MOVING AVERAGE CROSSOVER SYSTEMS?

A. *Set-ups based on situations where different MA's cross each other.* **Correct. These kind of systems are pretty popular, because they can give a fairly strong signal about trend acceleration or an upcoming trend reversal.**

B. *Moving Averages that are created by combining several Moving Averages which are crossing each other.* Nope.

C. *Trading systems based on Moving Averages that look a lot like Bollinger Bands, another technical indicator, hence the term 'Crossover'.* Sounds plausible, but unfortunately it's still hogwash.

QUESTION 30 WHAT IS THE MAIN STRENGTH OF THE RELATIVE STRENGTH INDEX?

A. *It filters out the noise of the market, because it shows the relative strength of a trend.* **Correct. The RSI compares the number of times the price closes higher with the number of times it closes lower. It also gives more weight to more recent data by using exponential averages. So, in effect it will give you more information about a trending movement than you would get from just looking at the trend line, because the RSI shows you whether the trend is growing weaker or stronger.**

B. *It shows the strength of a particular resistance/support level.* No, the RSI has nothing to do with this. On a side note, the strength of a resistance or support level can easily be spotted on a candlestick chart, by looking at how often a resistance/support level has already repelled an attack.

C. *That you can use it as a range trading tool.* Bollinger Bands are much more suitable as a range trading indicator, because they give insight into how often and by how much the price development is deviating from the channel. The RSI is better suited as a trend trading tool. Is the trend continuing? Is a trend reversal at hand? The Relative Strength Index can help you answer these kind of questions.

D. *That it shows where retracement will likely take place.* While this is something the RSI can help you with, it is but one of the movements the RSI can help you spot.

QUESTION 31 WHAT IS THE USE OF THE FIBONACCI SEQUENCE IN FOREX TRADING BASED ON?

A. *Nothing.* **The Fibonacci sequence is a series of numbers based on a mathematical rule. The number series has several distinct characteristics, for example that the ratio of connecting numbers is always 0,618. However, price development on the forex is created by human behavior, and traders base their trading on a lot of different factors. However, though the use of Fibonacci on the forex isn't based on anything mathematically or statistically valid, it still plays an important role. This is because many traders put a lot of faith in the 'Fibs', often turning them into a self-fulfilling prophecy. So you will encounter them often enough as a forex trader, but keep in mind there is no technical basis for them, only a psychological one.**
B. *The formula Fn = F(N-1) + F(n-2). The correct rule is Fn = F(n+1) + F(n-2).* Of course, the fact that the Fibonacci sequence is based on this rule, doesn't say anything about the validity of the Fibonacci sequence in forex trading.
C. *The Golden Ratio.* This is another word for the 0,68 ratio found between the series of numbers from the Fibonacci sequence.

About Part IV Forex Trading Strategies

QUESTION 32 PRICES ARE RANGING MORE OFTEN THAN THEY ARE TRENDING.
A. *True.* **Prices range about 70% – 80% of the time.**
B. *False.*

QUESTION 33 WHAT IS RETRACEMENT?
A. *A technique whereby the trader tries to find out how his trading system has progressed.* Finding out how your trading system performed is done by evaluating it. Has nothing to do with retracement.
B. *The partial retreat of a price after a significant rise or decline.* **Correct. The answer is kind of hidden in the meaning of the word of course, since 'retracement' means tracing back your steps. Retracement in trading is essentially the same thing, the price is retracing its earlier steps.**
C. *A set-up that seeks to repeat or copy a trade with one currency pair on another currency pair.* Nope.
D. *The breakout of a price development.* Also affectionately known as a 'breakout'. (go figure)

QUESTION 34 WHY IS TREND TRADING NOT FOR EVERYBODY?
A. *Because you need a hefty trading capital for it.* You don't necessarily need a lot of trading capital for trend trading, but you do need conservative money management.

B. *Because it's a fairly complex way of trading, too hard for beginners for example.* While you don't need a lot of technical skills and/or experience to be a good trend trader, you do need a certain set of skills and traits, such as resilience and stress resistance as well as a rational and analytical mind.

C. *Because it's often very hard to recognize a trend.* If ever there was something not hard in trading, it is recognizing a trend. However, successfully entering a trend and staying in it is a lot harder than it might seem.

D. *Because it usually means accepting a lot of small losses to produce one big winner, and not everybody can take that.* **This is indeed the main point about trend trading. Rationally speaking it's of course perfectly ok to be stopped out of 9 trades in a row for 30 pips a pop and win 1 trade worth 600 pips, but what if you actually have to suffer those 9 losing trades from up close and personal? Could you keep it together, or would you become frustrated, insecure, angry or depressed? Again, it's not for everybody.**

QUESTION 35 WHEN IS THE BEST TIME TO RANGE TRADE?

A. *When you have a lot of trading capital.* No, you don't need a particularly big bankroll to be able to range trade.

B. *During the European session.* The European session is usually the most volatile and unpredictable, because the largest part of the forex is concentrated in Europe. Ideally, the more predictable the better for a trader.

C. *When the market is relatively calm.* **This is the best time. You don't want any surprises and the least possible volatility. The more unrest, the greater the chance of spikes, kicking you out of your beautiful range trade.**

D. *Saturday.* Ehmm, well, no, because the forex is closed on Saturdays. (It's a good day for 0% losses though)

QUESTION 36 THE MORE TWO CURRENCIES ARE MUTUALLY DEPENDENT, THE MORE THEIR CURRENCY PAIR WILL BE RANGING.

A. *True.* **Indeed. When two currencies are mutually dependent, their currency pair will normally be fairly stable and mostly move in a tight range. Prices are already ranging more often than trending anyway, but with currency pairs like the EUR/CHF and the EUR/GBP it's even more common.**

B. *False.*

QUESTION 37 WHICH TECHNICAL INDICATOR WORKS BEST FOR RECOGNIZING A POSSIBLE RANGE TRADE?

A. *RSI.* The Relative Strength Index is more a tool for trend trading and breakout trading, because it's especially good at showing the relative strength of a trend.

B. *Exponential Moving Averages.* Another indicator that is better suited for trend trading and breakout trading.

C. *Simple Moving Averages.* The same as for A and B.

D. *Bollinger Bands.* **Yes, this is indeed a very good indicator when it comes to recognizing a possible range trade, because the BB's quickly show you whether or not price development tends to remain inside a channel.**

QUESTION 38 WHAT SHOULD YOU NEVER DO AFTER SETTING UP A RANGE TRADE?

A. *Chase the breakout when your stop loss is triggered.* Let's be honest, it can be very tempting to chase that breakout after you've just been stopped out of your range trade and the rate of the currency pair is running away like a wild stallion (or Black Beauty). But, most breakouts are false breakouts, and more often than not the price will return within the channel. The analysis you performed concluded the currency pair was possibly ranging. The fact that you have been just stopped out doesn't necessarily mean there is a breakout. The real reason you want to trade that breakout is because you don't want to accept your loss on the range trade and want to 'win' it back right away. (just like the average gambler in a casino). Don't give in to it.

B. *Use stop losses that are too tight.* Well, what is small? Obviously 'too' is never smart, but depending on your trading strategy it's feasible to use stop losses of just a couple of pips.

C. *Lose sight of the actual price development.* **When you plan your trade, set a profit target and a stop loss (with or without a trailing stop). After that you can play tennis or race in your Ferrari to you heart's content. No need to babysit your trade.**

D. *Put on a trend trade with another currency pair.* Nonsense of course. You can open positions for every currency pair you want, independent of range trades you have running on other currency pairs.

QUESTION 39 WHAT IS SCALPING?

A. *The tradition among forex traders to shave their heads if they have ended the year with a negative return on investment.* If this was your answer, you could already start shaving your head.

B. *A strategy whereby the whole trading capital is deployed in a single trade and the position is closed as soon as the profit is double the spread.* Strategy of champions, also known under its unofficial name 'widow maker'.

C. *Gradually 'growing' into a position, so as to limit the exposure risk.* A good strategy, but it has nothing to do with scalping.

D. *Keeping positions open only for a very short period, in order to quickly pick up small profits.* **Correct.**

QUESTION 40 IS SCALPING CONSIDERED A GOOD STRATEGY FOR BEGINNING

TRADERS?

A. *No, because it requires a lot of discipline and tolerance for stress.* **You could argue that not all beginning traders are created equal and that some beginners have remarkable discipline and are as tough as nails when it comes to stress. However, on the whole scalping is not an easy strategy for beginning traders. Speculating on the financial market is quite a mental challenge already, so why make it even more difficult by choosing a strategy that requires a high level of stress tolerance and could eat right through your trading capital with just a few badly timed tilts.**

B. *Yes, because it doesn't require an actual strategy, only good timing.* While this is certainly important, with scalping the one thing that is paramount is the ability to take a loss. Scalping is a relatively easy to understand trading strategy, but this should not be confused with it being easy to execute.

C. *Yes, because only small amounts of money are involved.* Nonsense. You can scalp for 10 cents a pip, but also for $10 a pip.

D. *No, because large amounts of money are involved.* It doesn't have a whole lot to do with that. A good scalper does not need that much trading capital at all, because a big percentage of his trades are winners – even if it's mostly only a couple of pips per trade – and his losing trades aren't that big either. With scalping, the trick is not to get carried away when a trade goes bad, and knowing when to close a winner.

QUESTION 41 WHAT IS BREAKOUT TRADING?

A. *Starting out with a new trading system.* Nope.

B. *Opening a position just as the price breaks through a resistance/support level.* **Correct. Bear in mind that most of these breakouts turn out to be false breakouts (a.k.a 'fakeouts') where prices return to a level below or above the previously broken resistance/support level.**

C. *Opening a position in the middle of a trend reversal.* It's very hard to identify a trend reversal right from the start. In hindsight it's easy of course, but when it is still forming it's hard to say – if not impossible – whether what you are seeing is the beginning of a trend reversal, or simply some retracement. What constitutes a trend reversal? Is it the breaking of an important support? An important resistance holding strong during an uptrend? When does retracement stop being retracement? Breakout trading, for that matter, is much more direct. There is a breakout when the price breaks through an important resistance/support. Opening a position at that moment, to profit from the rally, is called breakout trading

D. *Trading without a pre-planned strategy.* That's more like breakdown trading.

QUESTION 42 WHAT IS BREAKOUT FADING?

A. *Opening a position when the breakout seems to fail.* Since most breakouts fail, it makes sense to base a trading strategy on the failure of a breakout, which is exactly what breakout fading is about. However, you should not open a position at the first sign of breakout failure (unless you have very deep pockets). It could be just some temporary retracement, a breathing pause if you will, before the price storms on. To minimize risk it's therefore better to wait until the price has returned to the resistance/support it broke at the beginning of the breakout.

B. *Opening a position when the breakout transforms into a normal, solid trend.* This would have very little to do with 'fading', because there would be nothing to fade if the breakout succeeds.

C. *Opening a position when the breakout is over and the price has returned to the start of the breakout.* **Correct**.

D. *Closing a position that was based on a breakout.* This has nothing to do with fading the breakout either, because you traded the breakout and are now simply closing a position based on that breakout.

QUESTION 43 BREAKOUT FADING IS PRIMARILY MEANT AS A LONG TERM STRATEGY.

A. *True.*

B. *False.* **The chance of a successful breakout grows when it occurs on a chart that covers a longer period of time. In other words, a breakout on a weekly chart is more significant than one on a 5 minute chart. This implies that, conversely, fading a breakout – speculating it will fail – has more chance as a short term trading strategy.**

QUESTION 44 HOW DOES THE CARRY TRADE WORK?

A. *You buy a currency that carries a low interest and sell a currency that carries a high interest.* Unfortunately, it's the other way around.

B. *You sell a currency that carries a low interest and buy a currency that carries a low interest.* **The idea of the carry trade is based on profiting from the interest rate difference between two financial products, in this case currencies. For instance, if the interest on the Australian Dollar is 5% while it's only 0,1% for the Japanese Yen, you could earn 4,9% interest on a position by going short the Yen and long the Aussie.**

QUESTION 45 BELOW IS THE CANDLESTICK CHART FOR THE EUR/USD JUST AFTER THE NON-FARM PAYROLLS HAVE BEEN PUBLISHED, WHICH SHOW THAT EMPLOYMENT HAS RISEN MORE THAN EXPECTED. IS THIS A GOOD MOMENT TO GET IN ON THE EURO/USD?

A. *Yes, there is a clear, falling trend.* **What you're looking for when trading the news intra-day, is a clear signal that the news is pushing the price in one direction or the other. The effect of a news event like the publication** of the non-farms is usually the strongest during the first 30 to 60 minutes, so you have to get in quickly if you want to trade it.

B. *No. Although the price is falling, the period is much too short to speak of a trend, making a successful entry highly unpredictable.* If you're more comfortable trading with a longer horizon, you probably shouldn't trade economic news events like this. But for an intra-day trader, a clear signal on a 5 minute chart can be reason enough to get in on a trade.

C. *It's never wise to put on positions during these kinds of events.* Well, that's just your opinion...man.

D. *It's better to wait. Should the trend still be in place after an hour, it might be interesting to get in.* As said, that would be too long when trading economic events like this, because their direct impact often doesn't last more than an hour or so.

About Part V How to Become a Successful Forex Trader

QUESTION 46 WHY DO MOST BEGINNING TRADERS LOSE MONEY TRADING ON THE FOREX?

A. *Because they don't have a trading plan.*
B. *Because they lack realistic expectations.*
C. *Because they are unwilling to invest time and money.*
D. *All of the above.* **Easy question of course. Trading without a plan, without realistic expectations, without investing time and money, all three of them are recipes for the kind of forex cake that starts oozing bloated air the minute you prick the tiniest hole in it.**

QUESTION 47 IS SELF-ASSESSMENT IMPORTANT WHEN YOU WANT TO LEARN TO TRADE?

A. *No, not when you have a solid trading strategy.* Of course then the question remains how you got to that solid trading strategy in the first place.

B. *Yes, to find out what kind of trading system suits you best.* **There are many, many different trading systems and methods, and which one suits you best depends on how much time you have to trade, how much money you have and what kind of person you are. It is therefore important to first spend some time thinking about the parameters that define you as a trader, instead of immediately jumping into the deep end.**

C. *Not when you plan to use automated trading systems.* This is a common misconception. No matter how automated your system is, in the end you're still the one in control. Ultimately, you determine the parameters of your automated system, you decide how much trading capital the system can work with, how much profit can safely be extracted and how much of a loss you're willing to accept, just as you are the one who has to take steps to improve the system.

QUESTION 48 WHAT IS A SET-UP?

A. *A set of conditions that has to be met before a position is opened.* **Correct. You formulate your set-up in advance, and when all its conditions are met the set-up is said to have been triggered, after which you open the position.**

B. *Every trading strategy that uses Bollinger Bands.* While it is possible that Bollinger Bands are part of your strategy, they are not what defines a set-up.

C. *A trade that turns against you just before it touches your profit target.* Of course they should have reserved the term set-up for precisely this kind of incident; stabbed in the back by your trade just before the finish line, a real set-up! Instead it's used for the much more boring idea of a set of conditions that have to be met before the trade is triggered.

D. *A trade with a tight profit target.* No, it doesn't have anything to do with that.

QUESTION 49 WHAT IS MORE IMPORTANT, A GOOD EXIT STRATEGY OR A GOOD ENTRY STRATEGY?

A. *They are both equally important.* Both are indeed important, but a good exit strategy is nevertheless even more important. This is because it is primarily a bad or nonexistent exit strategy that gets you into trouble, as it can be responsible for unnecessarily large losses and unnecessarily small gains. A good exit strategy makes sure you set a good stop loss and formulate a clear profit target. This helps you to stay in and get out of a trade based on rational analysis not emotion.

B. *A good exit strategy.* **Correct.**

C. *A good entry strategy.* Again, a good entry strategy is important, but a good exit strategy has more potential to protect your trading capital and increase your profitability.

QUESTION 50 POSITION SIZING HAS NOTHING TO DO WITH RISK/REWARD RATIO.

A. *True.*

B. *False.* **Your position size – the percentage of your trading capital that you risk per trade – should be based partly on the ratio between winning and losing trades. The idea is that you can use a bigger position size when a higher percentage of your trades is profitable. You also need a positive expected value (EV) for every trade. For instance, when you risk $100 to win $1, you wouldn't even be profitable with a system that produces** winners 99% of the time. For every 100 trades, you would win an average 99 x $1 and lose 1x $100, for a total loss of $1; apart from the spread. Your profit expectation is determined by the chance for a winning trade and your risk/reward ratio. Based on a positive expected value and the percentage of winning trades, you can determine your maximum position size.

QUESTION 51 WHAT IS ONE OF THE MOST IMPORTANT GOALS OF POSITION SIZING?

A. *Maximizing profits.* These are dangerous words when trading the financial markets. Greed is good, yes, but never let it get in the way of solid risk management. If maximizing profit dictates taking on position sizes that increase your risk of ruin from 5 percent to 25 percent, would you do it?

B. *Minimizing the risk of ruin.* **This is indeed one of the most important goals. A good position size protects you against the inevitable downswings you'll face, because the market simply doesn't always do what you want it to. Bear in mind that even with a system that produces winners 75 percent of the time you could easily put on a 100 trades with only 30 winners. Your position size will protect you against these swings and keep you in the game.**

C. *To put on as many trades as possible at the same time.* No, the goal of position sizing is not to put on as many trades as possible. You could also wonder what would be the use of this, since most traders don't have a trading strategy that sends out a flood of triggered set-ups throughout the day.

D. *To make optimal use of your trading capital.* This is a little vague, because what would constitute 'optimum use'? Does it have to do with increasing profitability, decreasing losses, minimizing risk of ruin? Answer B is a better alternative here.

QUESTION 52 TRADER X HAS $500 IN TRADING CAPITAL AND RISKS $75 PER TRADE. HE JUST STARTED TRADING ON THE FOREX AND EXPECTS THAT HIS TRADING STRATEGY WILL PRODUCE A WINNING TRADE 60% OF THE TIME. CALCULATE HIS POSITION SIZE AND DECIDE IF IT IS ADEQUATE OR TOO RISKY.

A. *Position size is 15%, but this is too risky, it should be 6%.* **Correct. The position size is $75, on a total trading capital of $500. So trader X is risking 15% of his total trading capital on every trade. That's too much, because his trading strategy only produces a winner 60 percent of the time. (we're assuming his Expected Value is positive). The rule of thumb is that your position size should be no greater than 10% of your total percentage of winning trades, in this case 6%.**

B. *Position size is 15%, which is about the correct position size.* His position size is indeed 15%, but the risk of ruin is far too high here, because his percentage of winning trades is only 60%. Put differently, 6 back to back losing trades – not at all impossible – and he would not have enough capital to execute the same trade again. To be sure, 15% is almost always too big a position size since the risk of running 6 bad trades in a row is simply too big.

C. *Position size is 6%, which is about the correct position size.* The position size is not 6% in this case.

D. *There's not enough data to calculate the position size.* You only need to know the total trading capital and the exposure per position to be able to calculate the position size. You know both of them here.

QUESTION 53 WHEN A TRADER HAS AN EXPECTED VALUE OF $5,6 PER OPEN POSITION AND RISKS $24 PER POSITION, WHAT WOULD BE HIS EXPECTED VALUE EXPRESSED IN POSITION SIZE (EVP)?

A. *$5,6.*

B. *23 dollar cent.* **EVP shows the expected value per dollar risked. If you risk $24 with an EV of $5,6, that means that every risked dollar has an expected value of 23 cents**

C. *46 dollar cent.*

D. *There is not enough data to calculate the position size.* The position size is given, it's $24.

QUESTION 54 A GOOD RULE OF THUMB FOR THE MAXIMUM POSITION SIZE IS:

A. *1/5 of the total trading capital.* Also known as the 'Al-Qaeda' position size, because of its suicidal size.

B. *1/10 of the total trading capital.* A position size of 10%, a huge investment per trade. What if you have a system that produces a winner 50% of the time? (which can be a very profitable system, if you risk $1 to win $2). Imagine calling heads three times in a row and coming up tails every time. You've just lost 30% of your trading capital.

C. *1/10 of the total percentage of winning trades.* **One of the most important goals of your position size is to prevent you from going broke. Your position size therefore has to be able to protect you when you're in a rut. If you have a system that produces a winner only 15 percent of the time, you shouldn't have a position size of 5 percent. The reason is that it's statistically quite possible to underperform for quite a while. (keep in mind that the total percentage of winning trades is not the only thing that matters when it comes to determining your maximum position size -- expected value per trade is also important).**

D. *1/100 of your total trading capital.* That depends on your percentage of winning trades. A position size like that might be quite a good fit for a trend trading strategy that produces winners 10 percent of the time.

QUESTION 55 ARE THERE SITUATIONS WHEN YOU SHOULD NOT BE TRADING?

A. *There are several situations when you shouldn't be trading.* **No trader is always A-Ok, and for almost everybody it's better to stay away from trading when your mind is elsewhere.**

B. *Yes, for beginning traders there are, but experienced traders should be able to trade under all circumstances.* If you force yourself to this regime you'll be making it hard on yourself for no reason. Experienced traders usually will be quick to acknowledge that they don't trade when they can't bring their A game.

C. *That depends on your trading system.* In the end you are – or should be – at the center of every trading system you use, and it's also you who can change, tweak or bypass that system. Negative emotions will therefore always find a way into your trading if you trade when you are going through a rough patch.

QUESTION 56 IT IS NOT ALL THAT IMPORTANT TO READ FOREX BOOKS AND ARTICLES, AND PRACTICE A LOT, BECAUSE THE BEST FOREX TRADERS – THOSE UNDER 30 THAT HAVE ALREADY MADE MILLIONS FROM TRADING FOREX ONLINE – ARE PRIMARILY TRADING ON INSTINCT.

A. **False.**

B. *True.* Seriously? Then you must have been one of those persons who still believed in Santa Claus while your classmates where french kissing behind the principal's rose bushes.

C. *Maybe.* And....it's gone. Poof!

QUESTION 57 A SUCCESSFUL TRADER CAN CLOSE EVERY TRADE WITH A PROFIT.

A. *True.* No one is always on the right side of a trade, and it's not that important to begin with. You don't have to close every position with a profit to be profitable. If you only produce winners 25 percent of the time but risk only $30 to win $150, you would lose 3 x 30 = $90 and gain 1 x $150, for a total profit of $60 over 4 trades. That is an EV of $15 per trade, even though you only produce a winning trade 25 percent of the time.

B. **False.**

Bonus Questions

QUESTION 58 YOU ARE A BEGINNING TRADER AND HAVE PUT ON A POSITION TO SPECULATE ON THE EURO GOING HIGHER. YOU HAVE SET YOUR STOP LOSS AT 30 PIPS. AFTER ABOUT HALF AN HOUR THE TRADE IS VERY CLOSE TO YOUR STOP LOSS, BUT YOU HAVE A FEELING THE PRICE WILL STILL MAKE A TURN FOR THE BETTER.

WHAT DO YOU DO?

A. *A successful trader trades on instinct. Listen to your gut and move that stop loss down to give the trade more room.* That might be true for a very experienced trader, but not for a newbie who just arrived on the scene. Don't touch that stop and just accept your loss.

B. *See if there are news events supporting your gut feeling. If so, move up the stop loss.* If not, only move the stop loss if your gut feeling is unchanged. That's just searching for reasons not to have to take the hit. If you are looking for reasons to keep a trade open, you will always find them, because prices on the forex are influenced by a multitude of factors and contradicting opinions.

C. *Nothing.* **You're a beginning trader, not a seasoned vet who's trading instinct was developed back in the day, when 'iPhone' was nothing more than something a 3 year old might say. You don't know yourself as a trader well enough yet to be able to analyze your motivations rationally. For you, a novice trader, the stop loss should be sacred, something you worship as God's greatest gift to trading (well, one of 'm anyway)**

D. *Open a second trade, with the same target as the first. Leave the stop loss of the first trade unchanged.* Also known as cheating yourself. You leave the stop intact – so as not to break your rule of moving the stop loss when the trade turns against you – but opening the new trade has the same effect as moving the stop loss.

QUESTION 59 YOU ARE A DAY TRADER AND ARE HAVING A ROUGH DAY. YOU OPENED SIX TRADES EARLIER AND ALL SIX HAVE BEEN STOPPED OUT. YOU ARE PRETTY FRUSTRATED. WHAT DO YOU DO?

A. *Man up and open up six new trades.* You're frustrated and probably will not feel any better when opening six new trades that absolutely have to be winners. This is simply not the best time for you to trade. Just call it a day and go do something else.

B. *Man up, open six new trades and give them more room to breathe than the last six trades (i.e. put your stop loss further away).* If answer A was dumb, answer B is even dumber. You've just been stopped out six times in a row and your solution is to open six new trades right away and simply put the stop loss further away? Very clever, typical case of a trader that can't accept his loss. Just call it a day and go do something else.

C. *Call it quits for today.* **Exactly.**

QUESTION 60. YOU ARE A DAY TRADER. AN HOUR AGO YOU OPENED A POSITION BASED ON SOLID ANALYSIS, BUT NOTHING MUCH HAS HAPPENED SO FAR. THE PRICE WENT UP A LITTLE, DOWN A LITTLE, UP A LITTLE AGAIN , ETC. NEITHER YOUR STOP LOSS, NOR YOUR PROFIT TARGET HAVE COME EVEN CLOSE. WHAT DO YOU DO?

A. *Close the position and call it quits for today.* Why would you do that? Nothing has happened either way yet. Your set-up has neither been confirmed nor denied. That means you would just close the position out of, what, impatience? Bad reason.

B. *Nothing.* **A trader once said that watching prices develop was like watching paint dry. It's a slow process. Perhaps boring for some, but it is what it is. The fact that the price hasn't moved a lot is no reason to close the trade.**

C. *Close the position and go look for greener pastures.* There is no reason to do this. It's not about how fast you get there, but about getting there period.

APPENDIX III

EXPLANATION QUIZ SCORES

60 CORRECT ANSWERS

You are a forex god, surrounded by mere mortals! Let us learn from you. Backtesting, studying and evaluating your trading system are things you're probably doing already. Therefore, mentioning them is probably unnecessary, insulting even! You are the kind of forex talent that will likely go far.

52-59 CORRECT ANSWERS

Ok, so you're not a god just yet, but at the very least you are a forex prince, a natural with an innate sense of the different elements that are important when trading the forex. You could probably quit your job here and now and make an appointment with a bank to get a mortgage for a bigger house (don't forget to bring the results of this quiz to your appointment, to prove your exceptional trading talent)

45-51 CORRECT ANSWERS

Not bad at all. You know the basics, now is the time to go a little farther, so you can cash in on your knowledge. Read some more books and become active on one or more online forex forums, to speed your way up the learning curve.

35-44 CORRECT ANSWERS

Ok, you're definitely not a nitwit when it comes to forex trading, but you still have a lot of work to do. Perhaps you should read this book again and ask some questions on the forum of www.forexforambitiousbeginners.com about the parts you're having trouble with. Identifying your weak points and working on them will serve you well!

20-34 CORRECT ANSWERS

Back to school! Unfortunately, not everybody can be a winner on the trading floor. Read this book again, perhaps this time with your glasses on (or contacts in).

You shouldn't start with live trading yet (meaning with real money). Just open a demo account with a broker, so you can practice without risking your trading capital.

0-19 CORRECT ANSWERS

Ok, you definitely are a nitwit when it comes to forex trading. It is, I'll admit, quite an achievement to get so many questions wrong, but unfortunately there's no consolation price. Perhaps you were a bit (or very) drunk while answering the questions, or maybe you thought it was a dating quiz or something, fact is that you did terrible.

Since this is a free country (and I hope yours is too) no one can stop you from trading, but perhaps we should make an exception for people like you – just for your own protection. Even trading with a demo account is inadvisable, because although there would be only play money involved, you will likely find a way to lose real money anyway.

APPENDIX IV

SHORT FOREX LEXICON

OPENING A POSITION

This means buying or selling one or more lots. For example, you can open a position on the forex by buying 1 mini lot EUR/USD.

LONG OR SHORT

Whenever you want to speculate that a currency will rise in value, you go long that currency. Conversely, speculating it will fall is called going short (also called shorting) the currency.

STOP LOSS

This is a predetermined price – somewhere below the break-even point – at which a position will be closed, to prevent further losses. For instance, suppose you buy 1 lot GBP/USD at $1,6250 and place a stop loss at $1,6180, your maximum loss would be 70 pips. In other words, a stop loss enables you to determine, in advance, exactly how much of a loss you're willing to take on a given position. Especially as a beginner, you should always put in a stop loss.

TAKE PROFIT

A predetermined price – somewhere above the break even point – at which a position will be closed, to take profit. It works the same as a stop loss, only in this case the position is moving in your favor. Many traders put in a take profit (a.k.a a profit target) to prevent them from exciting too soon out of fear, or too late, out of greed. Putting in a take profit is not as essential as putting in a stop loss, but beginners would generally do well to use the take profit option, because it trains you to trade according to a predetermined plan – which is one of the most important prerequisites for being successful as a trader.

BULLS & BEARS

Traditionally, the nickname for traders who think the market will go up is 'bulls', while those that think the market is going down are called 'bears'. It's therefore no coincidence that there is a statue of a big, bronze bull on the Wall Street Square in New York City; it symbolizes belief in the 'bullishness of capitalism'.

BID AND ASK

The broker always offers two rates for a currency pair, the bid and ask. The bid – always the lowest of the two – is the price for selling or shorting a currency pair. The ask price tells you against what price you can buy the currency pair. The difference between the two rates is called the spread.

SPREAD

The difference between the bid and ask price, which is pocketed by the broker for services rendered (namely opening the position for you). So when the bid price for the EUR/USD is 1,4000 and the ask price is 1,4003, the spread is 3 pips.

BASE CURRENCY / QUOTE CURRENCY

As said, currencies are always traded in pairs. You can trade the euro against the dollar, against the pound, the yen, etc. The currency first mentioned in a currency pair is called the base currency. This is the currency that you're de facto buying when you buy a Lot. When you buy one Lot EUR/USD for instance, it means you go long the euro. The second currency, in which the base currency is expressed, is called the quote currency. For the currency pair EUR/USD, the dollar is therefore the quote currency and the value of the euro is expressed in dollars.

CROSS CURRENCIES

These are currency pairs where the US Dollar as neither base nor quote currency. Examples are the EUR/GBP, EUR/JPY, GBP/JPY. Because these currency pairs are less liquid (meaning they are traded less often) their spread is higher.

CANDLESTICK CHART

The most popular way of tracking a currency pair's price development is using a candlestick chart. It consists of 'candles' in two colors (usually red and green), one to signify a period of price rise, the other a period of price decline. The lowest point of the candle shows the lowest price reached during the period, the highest point of the candle shows the highest price reached. A green candle means that the price closed at the high end of the body (thick part) of the candle, a red candle means the price closed at the low end of the body.

Legend has it that the candlestick chart was invented in the seventeenth century by a Japanese rice trader who was looking for a better way to quickly gain insight into the price development of, well, rice.

Volumes have been written about the different patterns that can be discerned from candlestick charts. You will therefore have no trouble getting your fill If you would like to know more about the Three White Soldiers, the Ichumu cloud and other wonderful chart patterns which sound like they come out of an adult version of Pokémon.

LEVERAGE

Leverage is the ratio between the underlying value of a transaction and the amount of money that is actually being reserved to cover losses. This makes speculating on a financial instrument much easier for traders with only a small trading capital, because they only need a fraction of the total amount of money they are controlling.

Example: using leverage of 400:1 – the maximum leverage at most forex brokers – you would only need $2,50 in available funding to open 1 micro lot EUR/USD.

1 micro lot = 1000 units

leverage 400:1

Available funding needed = 1000/400 = $2,50

Because a pip is 10 cents when buying micro lots, $2,50 will buy you a buffer of 25 pips that the price can move against your position (before it's automatically closed). Put differently, with 400:1 leverage you can control $1000 worth of currency with an investment of only $2,50.

Leverage is a double-edged sword of course, because it magnifies losses as well as profits. It's also what opens up the forex market to smaller traders, who want to trade the financial market more aggressively and thus pursue higher profits.

STANDARD LOT

A unit of measure that represents 100,000 units of any currency. This original measure has since been joined by the Mini Lot (10,000 units) and the Micro Lot (1,000 units).

PIP

The smallest measured price change for a currency pair. The fourth number behind the decimal point for most currency pairs (for example, for the EUR/USD: $1.4522).

RESISTANCE / SUPPORT

Price levels a currency pair had trouble breaking in the past or that form a natural barrier, like the psychological $1,5000 level for the EUR/USD

Resistance points are price levels a rising currency pair has trouble breaking. The more often the rally of a currency pair is stopped at a specific resistance level, the stronger that resistance level is said to be.

The same goes for support, but in this case with falling prices.

APPENDIX V

BIBLIOGRAPHY